Challenging Children
A Puzzle
To Be
SOLVED

Stories from
Parent's Who Were Empowered by the
Whole Child Institute

by Linda Vettrus & Mary Topero with Lisa Ragsdale

A reference guide that reveals the importance of early intervention and explores the relationship between nutrition and body brain connection, advocacy and survival, toxicity and health, movement and learning. These stories were written by parents who have received helpful guidance from the Whole Child Institute.

"These stories were compiled in order to help parents and professionals explore various cause and core reasons why we are seeing such an increase of high needs children today."

—Dr. Keith Sehnert, M.D.

To Order
Send $20.00 to the

Whole Child Institute–WCI

e-mail: wcichild@yahoo.com
651-246-9288
www.WholeChildInstituteWCI.com
The Whole Child Institute became an LLC
June 30, 2005

Library of Congress Card Catalog Number 97-072917
ISBN 0-9654714-1-1

Published by the Whole Child Institute–WCI under the
supervision of Lisa C. Ragsdale.

Printed by Bang Printing in Brainerd, MN.

Cover Design by Gabriel Christopher Dee.
Logo Artwork by Jane Martin
Design by Linda Vettrus

Text entry by Lisa C. Ragsdale and Linda Vettrus.

Appendix IV, data entry by Debby Lineer.

Editing by Lisa C. Ragsdale and Linda Vettrus.

Whole Child Institute—WCI
Favorite Sayings

"The doctor of the future will give no medicine, but will interest his patients in the care of the human frame, in diet and in the cause and prevention of disease"

—Thomas Alva Edison

"What you're not up on, you're down on,"
As the old saying goes!

"To know, truly is to know by causes"

—Bacon

"Happy is he who knows the reason for things"

—Virgil

"Let thy food be thy medicine."

—Hippocrates

"Where the sun does not enter, the doctor does."

—Italian Proverb

"You must do things you think you cannot do."

—Eleanor Roosevelt

"You may have to fight a battle more than once
to win it."

—Margaret Thatcher

"There are no mistakes in life, only valuable
learning experiences."

—Linda Vettrus

"Teaching kids to count is fine, but teaching them
what counts is best."

—Bob Talbert

Prayer for the Day

"So far today, God, I've done alright. I haven't
gossiped, I haven't lost my temper, I haven't been
grumpy, nasty or selfish. I'm really glad of that, but in
a few minutes, I'm going to get out of bed; and from
then on, I'm probably going to need a lot of help."

—Author Unknown

Acknowledgements

This book is dedicated to our families and to all families. We are grateful to our husbands, Greg Vettrus and Bill Topero for their support and encouragement.

Thank you dear husbands for giving us "hibernation time" to retreat and write this book.

We have our children to thank—Dan, Amy, Thomas, Eric, and Steven for inspiring the mission and passion for which this book was written. Without them in our lives, this book would never exist.

We appreciate this opportunity to thank all the families who contributed their stories. We would also like to thank our many volunteers who spent time reading, editing, and supporting us in various ways.

We are especially grateful to Lisa Ragsdale for her loving support, encouragement, and constancy as the guiding writer of this book.

We are grateful to all the families who made their way to the Whole Child Institute and entrusted us to help them make positive changes. We are also thankful to you, the reader, for the desire to educate yourself so that you, too, can make a difference.

Disclaimer

This book is a compilation of stories about families who were helped by the Whole Child Institute. The authors have written this book in order to help parents make educated choices for their children and to heighten their awareness to look beyond symptoms to *why* their child may have these symptoms. Upon uncovering the *why,* parents have a better understanding as to what they should do next. This is not a detailed book on set protocols or specific therapies, but a beginning reference source for parents and other professionals.

Each story is an individual case as the Whole Child Institute helped that family make educated choices. Many of the names have been changed at the request of various families. The authors want to warn parents, that because each child is unique, they should not try to duplicate any one treatment for their child without the guidance of a physician or licensed healthcare professional.

This book is not intended to provide personal medical advice or treatment, or to be a substitute for medical care. The publisher and authors are not responsible for any adverse effects or consequences resulting from the use of therapies discussed in this book. This book is not intended to encourage parents to take their child off medication, but to help them make informed choices.

Any changes to diet or health care for the reader or their child should be thoroughly discussed with a personal physician.

"Never tamper, stop, or alter your own or your child's medications without specific guidance or advice from a personal physician."

—Dr. Doris Rapp, M.D.

Preface

All children can be challenging from time to time. Children with learning and/or behavioral problems can create challenges beyond the norm. Do any of theses challenges sound familiar?

Impulsive, predictably unpredictable, unable to follow the rules, easily distracted, sloppy/disorganized, lacks self-discipline, wastes time arguing, inappropriate social skills, needs one-to-one supervision in order to complete a task, works beneath ability level, average to above average intelligence, hears—but does not always seem to process the message, feels overwhelmed, aggressive behavior, lacks motivation, difficulty relating positively to siblings, peers, and/or authority figures, highly sensitive to clothing, light and sound, dislikes drinking water and/or eating a healthy diet, no label or "ABC Kid" label (see glossary for "ABC Kid" definition).

Children who are challenging can be found in every culture and community and are in need of individualized assessments and attention. Looking at the whole child and all of the pieces of their complex puzzle, helps parents go beyond symptoms deeper into the cause and core of their frustrations.

As in the video movie Lorenzo's Oil, these are stories of parents on a search in order to understand what is happening inside their child and how to improve or reverse a downward spiral.

At the Whole Child Institute we encourage others to look at the "whole child" in order to resolve academic failure. We empower parents to make informed choices, while providing good nutrition for their own bodies as well as our most precious resource, our children.

Foreword

Dr. Keith Sehnert, M.D.

I have known and worked with the co-founders of the Whole Child Institute, Linda Vettrus and Mary Topero for several years. The education, research and experience they have brought to the Institute is first rate. As special education teachers and mothers, they earned "Ph.D.s" in the "College of Hard Knocks." Each has had the experience of having challenging children of their own. They learned first hand how little help is available for parents. Most of the help offered was made on the assumption that the "trouble" they were experiencing with their children was "all in their heads." Through their own experiences and that of others they've worked with, they've gained a great deal of information and insight to offer parents of children who are challenging, behaviorally, emotionally, and academically.

The advice and counseling that Mary and Linda received as parents overlooked the fact that many of the <u>psychological</u> symptoms children exhibit have a <u>physiological</u> origin. I am referring to such things as hidden food allergies to common foods, environmental allergies to dust, chemicals, and other toxins, or yeast/candida infections caused by the use of broad spectrum antibiotics. These and other "modern medical mysteries" such as vitamin and nutritional deficits may be a factor in ADD/ADHD and similar behavioral disorders discussed in this book.

When my own daughter, Cindy, was a newborn in the hospital, there was an outbreak of staph infection in the nursery. Six babies, including Cindy, were infected. One child even died. Cindy was given the broad-spectrum antibiotic, Streptomycin (now off the market.) It killed the infection but also "killed" her

i

hearing and she became deaf. What followed during her childhood was a series of chronic yeast infections, thrush and vaginitis. It took many years to cleanse her body of an overgrowth of candida yeasts, using a low-sugar diet, avoiding milk and other dairy products. Special education was needed to deal with her hearing loss. Today she is a college graduate and "working mom" with two wonderful daughters, Juliana and Heather. Her husband "J.J." also deals with a hearing impairment and works in Kansas City, MO with people who deal with disabilities.

As a medical doctor, much of my work has been in antibiotic awareness and some of the problems caused by over use. You'd be surprised at how much I have suffered from merely trying to tell people that there are a lot of other ways to get well rather than taking antibiotics for everything that comes along. Things are changing now, but there still are a majority of doctors who say, "This is the way it has always been done, so therefore your way is wrong." Although it takes about twenty five years to make a paradigm shift, American doctors are beginning to think twice before prescribing an antibiotic. Some are even prescribing probiotics to be taken with the antibiotic and for several weeks following antibiotic treatment. This protocol helps balance the intestinal flora. In other words allows the immune system to heal the body. Throughout history, there have been paradigm shifts or changes in traditional thinking due to an increase in knowledge of scientific factors, economic changes, competition, or new social, religious, and political ideas. For example, Martin Luther went to the Pope, the highest authority of the Catholic Church, and asked if the communion service could be given in German. The Pope declined, and Martin Luther was threatened that he would be jailed if he continued to express his ideas by suggesting a change in the status quo. With his persistence over time, however, the Protestant religions were created. Galileo suggested to his contemporaries that the earth was round, not flat and that the sun was the center of the universe. He hypothesized that the earth rotated around the sun and not the sun around us. He was basically run out of town, because his ideas did not concur with current thinking. When his theory was scientifically investigated it was found to be true and people changed their thinking. These are examples of paradigm shifts, or changes in traditional thinking that happen over time. As I mentioned before, such a shift generally takes an average of twenty-five years from the time it is suggested until it is finally realized and recognized as acceptable to mainstream society. The Whole Child Institute is part of a paradigm shift in health care that we are noticing today.

> **"Great spirits have always faced violent opposition from mediocre minds."**
>
> **—Albert Einstein**

People are more likely to consider alternative health care these days than they were just a few years ago as more and more they are becoming disillusioned with traditional medical therapy. Patients are frustrated that many doctors prescribe medications that have harmful side effects, cover up symptoms, and do not address the cause and core of an illness. Some medical doctors seem to have forgotten the meaning of the phrase they recited in the Hippocratic Oath, "First, do no harm." The alternative methods used by the Whole Child Institute reflect the philosophy of this important statement. There are no invasive procedures involved in the Whole Child Assessment, and children are made to feel comfortable and accepted for who they are. The Institute offers a host of auxiliary services provided by professionals such as massage, counseling, hair analysis, food allergy/sensitivity testing, environmental analysis, CranioSacral Therapy, Ersdal Zone Therapy, and Kinetic/Therapeutic Education. Looking at the entire person, a plan is put together which specifically meets an individual's needs. Investigation into the cause and core of a child's problems, nutritional and environmental counseling, as well as implementing unique methods for learning, are essential parts of the services of the Whole Child Institute. The WCI has made a big difference for many children and their families. It could make a difference for yours.

Keith W.Sehnert, M.D.
Author of sixteen books, including *How To Be Your Own Doctor Sometimes, Stress/Unstress and his latest book Dr. Sehnert's New Guide for Stress Management.* Former professor at Georgetown University, Washington, D.C. and the acclaimed "George Washington" of medical self-care in working with children and their parents.

The Whole Child Institute
helps parents
make
educated choices!

Chapters

Chapter One:
Whole Child Institute..............................1

Chapter Two:
Children Who Are Challenging....................8

Chapter Three:
Desperation To Victory...........................16

Chapter Four:
Early Intervention.................................23

Chapter Five:
Sensory Integration Processing...................29

Chapter Six:
Auditory Integration Processing..................37

Chapter Seven:
Visual Integration Processing..................47

Chapter Eight:
The Key To Healthy Choices.....................54

Chapter Nine:
Our Toxic World....................................61

Chapter Ten:
Total Nutrition.............................…..............74

Chapter Eleven:
A New Horizon......................................83

Chapter Twelve:
Light At The End Of The Tunnel...................87

Chapter Thirteen:
Out With The Bad—
In With The Good.............................91

Chapter Fourteen:
Overcoming Abuse,
Depression & Toxicity.........................98

Chapter Fifteen:
"Mom, I Just Want To Learn!"...................104

Chapter Sixteen:
Instilling the Love of Learning and The
Self-Taught Child—
The Kumon Philosopy...................106

Chapter Seventeen:
"I Do Have Control!"............................115

Chapter Eighteen:
  At Last Success In School.......................118

Chapter Nineteen:
  Balancing Children For Success.................124

Chapter Twenty:
  Slow Down and Take Time
          To Enjoy Your Child........................158

Chapter Twenty-one:
  Camye's Story.......................…..........164

Chapter Twenty-two:
  Helping Families
          With Children Who Are Challenging 171

People First Language...........................174

Puzzle Pieces.......................………....176

Appendix I: *Whole Child Institute*

Appendix II: *Organizations*

Appendix III: *Glossary*

Appendix IV: *Books*

          A. *Nutritional*
          B. *Educational*
          C. *Resources for Patterned Learners*

Chapter One

*Motto: Looking at the whole child while resolving
academic failure in America today!*

Co-founders of the Whole Child Institute, Linda Vettrus and Mary Topero are both mothers and educators of children with academic and behavioral challenges. Both women hold Minnesota State Teaching Licenses in Special Education. Each of these women separately began a long frustrating road years ago in search of help for their own children. As a result of their pursuit of information they became a clearing-house of practical resources which are least costly and least invasive for treating a challenging child. In April of 1994, they co-founded Empowering Parents of Challenging Children, then in 1997 they changed the name to the Whole Child Institute. They pooled their resources so that other parents wouldn't have to go through the frustrations they went through. Linda and Mary offered one-of-a-kind help for parents when children were challenging. Their shared goal was healthy kids and healthy families!

Linda and Mary provided classes and workshops for a variety of audiences, which included parents, educators, psychologists and child-care providers. They taught winning strategies for dealing with children labeled ADD/ADHD, EBD, ODD, etc. They taught at the Minnesota School of Professional Psychology for their Continuing Education Program and Community Education classes for various Twin City school districts. They also produced videos and participated in interviews for public television and radio. Due to the efforts of Linda Vettrus and Mary Topero, everyone who came in contact with the Whole Child Institute came away with new and helpful information.

Whole Child Institute

The Whole Child Institute now serves parents and their children, helping them figure out why their child is not learning, or behaving in a certain way, perhaps showing symptoms under various labels. Is it a lack of enough pure water in their diet? Is it a food sensitivity? Is it boredom? Is it that he just learns in a different way? Having an informal whole child assessment gives parents the "biggest bang for their buck." It is a practical way to discover what is really going on with a child before trying medication, or sticking a label on a child whom isn't really suffering from a medical or psychological problem. The assessment is based on the research, knowledge and experience of the co-founders as well as that of experts in the field of preventive medicine, brain research, and accelerated learning.

Parents who are willing to look at the **whole** child benefit the most from an assessment, which considers biochemical, nutritional, social, emotional, physical and mental needs. A Whole Child Assessment is designed to pinpoint possible problems with visual, auditory, and sensory integration processing, as well as to explore temperament traits, "The Seven Intelligences," levels of toxicity, the learning byte, and much more. Parents provide a brief history of their child's developmental progress, school performance, past/present health, how she interacts with others, and how she feels about learning, etc. During a whole child assessment, parents are able to discover the cause and core of a child's difficulties. Rather than dealing with symptoms, parents are able to address the reasons for the challenges they are facing. Towards the end of an assessment a realistic plan of action is set forth. This action plan serves as a guide which helps parents through the maze of information and resources they may not realize are available.

A very important part of the whole child assessment is checking for food sensitivities and identifying culprits in a child's diet, which may be causing behavioral and/or learning problems. The client is screened for sensitivities to certain kinds of water, artificially sweetened drinks, meats, poultry, fish, grains, and processed products such as crackers, commercially packaged dishes, dairy products, eggs, canned vegetables and fruits, organic and non-organic food items and condiments. Testing is also done for metal toxicity and sensitivity to environmental pollutants such as tobacco smoke, chemical pollutants, dust-mites, pollens, mold and even air fresheners. Kinesiology is used to discover the truth about how a child feels concerning a particular subject in school, or related things like homeschooling, being part of a class, or even their present teacher.

Looking at the body from a chemical/nutritional point of view has been beneficial in understanding various special needs labels, which are so freely given to children these days. For some children their ADD is caused by a blood sugar imbalance and for others ADHD occurs when that imbalance is so extreme that the adrenal glands need to overproduce in order to keep a very toxic, suppressed system up and running. Certain children can work out of such a label with consistent, proper nutritional and biochemical treatments balanced with learning and occupational therapies.

At the Whole Child Institute, parents are taught that consistency is the key to a stable environment. Consistent rules, consistent discipline, consistent monitoring of the environment (music, books, magazines, television, diet, supplements, etc.) Having a routine adds stability to the life of a child.

Children, especially those with learning and/or behavioral challenges, cannot tell you why they react to life the way they do—they do not know. The staff at the Whole Child Institute, feel it is necessary to create an environment for opportunity and help parents remove some of the major obstacles that stand in the way of their child's success.

<u>About the Authors</u>

It seems that ***Linda Vettrus*** was destined to become a Special Education teacher. She has always been a creative person who enjoys working with children. At the age of twelve she and a friend set up a summer school for preschool children and a neighborhood club for elementary age children. They had about ten children for the preschool program and approximately fifteen for their junior club. The preschoolers learned songs, stories, played games and even put on a parade. The junior club held a rummage sale and paid for a field trip with their earnings. They also participated in learning games, crafts and picnics.

Linda has a long history of working with children dealing with a variety of challenges. The summer following the junior club experience, she was employed by the parents of a junior club member to be the caregiver for their, seven year old, daughter with diabetes and was responsible for carefully monitoring her diet and physical activities. While a dance instructor for six years at a local dance studio she taught a child who had epilepsy. A friend of the family had a ten year old daughter who was blind and dealing with Autism. As a highschooler, Linda taught her how to walk up and down the steps outside their home. While in college, Linda befriended a foster child of her great aunt and uncle who was legally blind and developmentally disabled. This brief relationship and a fifteen hour a week internship in a learning center for students with learning disabilities (through Normandale Community College in Bloomington, MN) led Linda into the field of Special Education.

While attending St. Cloud State University in Minnesota, Linda formed her ideas about education. She believes that a teacher must be aware of individual differences in his or her students. The organization of a classroom should be flexible, allowing students some freedom while teaching them how to manage change and develop an awareness of time. She feels it is important to treat students as children and not as miniature adults. She comments, "Curriculum should be based on activities that serve as an object lesson, relating the information to real world experiences." Mastery of the basics and accelerated foundational learning give her students a competitive edge.

Linda holds a bachelor's degree in Special Education. Her work history includes being an educator of the developmentally disabled population and part time group home staff member. She was an Educational Consultant for Discovery Toys for more than fifteen years and is a Kumon Math and Reading franchise owner. Linda has homeschooled gifted children dealing with ADD/ADHD, Autism, Manic Depression, Dyslexia, Dysgraphia, and Dyscalculia. She is also familiar with ODD, OCD, and EBD behaviors, (see glossary for definitions.)

Mary Topero had wanted to be a teacher ever since she was in second grade. In 1969 she started teaching as a first grade teacher and continued for five years. At that point, she felt directed to take Montessori training, so she retired from public school education and took Montessori training for one year. She taught for one year in a Montessori Academy in Southern California. She then met her husband and for the next twelve years they raised their children while Mary worked as a substitute teacher in Special Education.

When she was offered a position as a substitute teacher for young children with physical disabilities who didn't have mental involvement, she realized she had found her niche. Mary went back to school and received her POHI license in order to teach students with Physical and Other Health Impairments, which now includes children with Attention Deficit Disorder and Attention Deficit Hyperactivity Disorder. She moved from California to Richfield, Minnesota in 1989 and worked part-time as a consultant for an intermediate school district that services the regular school districts for their low-incidence populations. "Low incidence" means children with high needs, but who are not disciplinary problems. As a consultant, she would go out to various school districts to advise teachers and work one-on-one with the children.

Mary's reasons for co-founding the Whole Child Institute are very personal. She has three sons with personalities, unique and challenging each in his own way. Mary believes her youngest son, Steven, is the real reason she has been called to empower parents of children who can be more challenging than their siblings or peers. Ever since Steven was very young, he has been living with such labels as ADD, ADHD, EBD and ODD. In her search for answers and praying for ways to help him, she was led to share what she's learned with other parents, first on an informal basis, and then through co-founding the Whole Child Institute.

With over twenty years of teaching experience, Mary holds a bachelor's degree in Child Development and Family Life. She holds a Minnesota State Teaching License in Elementary Education. She is POHI certified (Physically and Other Health Impaired, including Attention Deficit Disorders.)

Linda Vettrus and Mary Topero created the Whole Child Institute out of their love for children and their families in order to help them along a journey they have traveled themselves. They began their mission helping families towards natural alternatives to medication and innovative techniques for teaching children struggling with behavioral and/or learning problems. With an estimated 1.5 million children now on medication for ADD/ADHD, the Whole Child Institute offers education, resources and solutions on the cutting edge of academics and alternative healthcare.

Mary has entrusted Linda Vettrus with their mission to empower parents and is no longer with the Whole Child Institute. Mary is currently working in the field of Health Kinesiology and teaches classes concerning the health benefits of essential oils.

The New, Whole Child Institute

Linda Vettrus is the Director of the Whole Child Institute—WCI. Assessments are provided by appointment and include a written plan of action based on the results of testing by the various professional who are involved at the whole child assessment. Volunteers are always needed to guide parents on their journey once they have an established plan of action. The Whole Child Institute does not promote any one product, organization, or professional and pursues a continual search for the least costly, yet most effective, highest quality products and services. The Whole Child Institute offers educational tools and strategies which meet the specific needs of all learners.

**Looking at the whole child while
resolving academic failure
in America today!**

**The WCI offers whole child assessments,
least invasive resources, as well as
tools and strategies which
meet the needs of
all learners.**

Chapter Two

This story helps to explain the genetic factor for children with behavioral challenges. Linda Vettrus, co-founder and director of the Whole Child Institute shares her story.

"I can accept and understand my children better, when I think back through my heritage. My paternal grandmother was such a challenging child, that her parents were forced to send her back to 'the states' from their mission field in South America. Her son, my father, was a handful. He was a daredevil from the get-go, and was diagnosed with Manic Depression when I was four years old. He received shock therapy at the VA hospital in Minnesota and was sent home in remission, which lasted approximately thirteen years. He died of a successful suicide attempt the summer before my senior year of high school. We were very close and I missed him more than words can say.

My maternal grandmother used to tell me stories about my mother when she was little. 'Little' is the operative word. She was so small that at age three, she wore clothes that would fit an eighteen-month old baby. She was strong-willed and could outsmart her older brother any day of the week.

Sibling rivalry was at its finest in that household. As a teenager, her job was to vacuum and dust. When it came to doing her brother's room, he made her push his 'doorbell' which by the way, had a pin in it. She would push it so as to avoid the pinprick, and then say, 'Ouch!' Thinking she had been pricked by the pin, he would beam with joy and let her in. Although my maternal grandmother told me stories about my mom and how difficult she was when she was young, I didn't appreciate them until I had my own 'little darlings.' Then we would have debates in order to decide who had been the most challenging child. My son usually took first place, my mother second, and I usually landed in third.

I've discovered there were several puzzle pieces that fit together revealing why we had all been so challenging. I was told I used to eat newspaper and dirt, which may have been a sign of a mineral deficiency. As a preschooler, I bit an oral thermometer and little balls of mercury went everywhere, possibly even inside of me!

My tonsils were removed in second grade and my appendix was removed while I was in high school. At that point, my bacterial collecting organs were now gone.

As a teenager, I had acne so bad my dermatologist put me on Tetracycline, which I later discovered fed Candida yeasts in my lower intestine. These yeasts multiplied, excreting toxins that weakened my immune system. This 'leaky gut' syndrome caused by the Candida, led to my many food sensitivities. I now know that acne and a toxic liver are related. Rather than my taking an antibiotic for acne a simple liver detoxification protocol could have saved me ill health in later years.

Although I was exhausted during my first pregnancy, I was delighted at the prospect of becoming a parent. As a special education teacher, I knew I could make a difference with this child. What I didn't know is that this child was going to make a difference in *me*.

Dan was an exceptionally easy newborn and was sleeping eight hour nights, not to mention two three-hour naps per day. I was actually bored for the first time in my life! The boredom soon disappeared as I watched Dan's amazing 'firsts' come way ahead of schedule. He was born with a very mature nervous system, and held his head up at birth. He lifted his head off the bed when he was a day old. By the third day, he almost flipped off the changing table and by six and-a-half weeks, he could roll from his tummy to his back. He smiled when he was two weeks old. At eight weeks he was grabbing glasses off of people's faces. My husband and I began to wonder just how much of a 'stinker' he was going to be. When he was twelve weeks old, he began to develop a temper, and he did not do well sleeping anywhere but at home or in the car. He disliked being held and would even twist and turn while sitting in his stroller. His teeth came in early and he started jabbering at five months of age. Before he was even seven months old, he could say, 'Hi, Hi Da, Dada, Dadee, Mama, and Bow Wow.' I remembered he had done many things very early, but when I checked his baby book before writing this chapter, I hadn't remembered just how early they had been. By the time he was a year old he was speaking in simple sentences. For example he would say, 'A ball, Mom' (while holding one out to me.) 'A bottle, Mom.' 'Hold this.' 'Hold that.' His walking and crawling abilities developed within the average range.

Dan had his first cold at nine weeks and his first ear infection at four months, which was treated with an antibiotic. He needed a lot of sleep, eleven hours at night and five hours worth of naps during the day. He would get extremely hyperactive when he was tired. At these times he ran on nerves; his and mine. At seven-and-a-half months, Dan had the worst ear infection of his life. He was as weak and limp as a premature baby. He was so feverish that if I held him, his temperature would go up. He could only take an ounce of formula an hour. I also had an ear infection at the same time and got sicker just trying to take care of him. Being sick became a routine occurrence between the two of us.

His activity level increased and by eight-and-a-half months of age, even though he wasn't walking, he was already climbing. He soon began to climb stairs like greased lightning. He would unplug the telephone while, mommy was talking, and even flush the toilet. He became a miniature Houdini getting out of his carseat, and only stayed in it if he felt like it. I was thankful he was still somewhat obedient at that point in time, and would usually choose to stay restrained. Car rides were out of the question on his bad days, unless it was 'nap time'. Dan loved to sleep in the car.

He was smart as a whip and was playing board games with me by the time he was eighteen months old. Thank God for Discovery Toys! I became an Educational Consultant so I could keep Dan stimulated. I learned more by being involved with Discovery Toys than I did getting my degree in Special Education.

Dan continued to develop and when he was two and a half, I knew it was time for preschool. My mother came to babysit so I could go sign him up. He was supposedly napping. As I left the house, two vaporizers came tumbling out of the attic window. Guess who wasn't sleeping yet?

His sister Amy was an annoyance to him even before she was born. I was in the hospital in premature labor with her the day of Dan's second birthday so he had to have his birthday celebration at the hospital with only his daddy and me. When she was finally born two months later, he was delighted and enjoyed being a big brother. Although he loved his sister, Dan was always 'after' her. I wasn't always sure how to keep her alive!

Dan's over-activity began to change our social life. One evening, when he was three I invited a close friend and her husband over for dinner. Dan's behavior became unruly and I had to put him in his room with the tot-lock™ on the door. The minute I got back downstairs, there were toys raining past the dining room window. We had combination windows with spring tabs that had to be moved towards each other, while sliding the heavy glass up; this had to be repeated in order to get the screen up. Somehow, he was able to do this himself and began tossing toys out his window. One day, with two tugs on the chained front door, he managed to pull the oak door frame out of the plaster wall just enough so he could slip outside. He often had displays of 'super human' strength.

Dan's speech and language skills began to decrease. Even though at two, if someone didn't understand what he meant, he would rephrase his sentences. He became anti-social at playgroup. One day we had to leave because all he would do is throw sand at the other kids. I remember that day well, because we both sat on the front steps and cried.

When he was two I took him to a child guidance clinic to get some help. He was assessed and I was told that if he was driving me that crazy, I might want to put him on Ritalin. In my motherly gut, I knew that you didn't put a sick child on Ritalin. I wasn't sure what that meant until Dan was ten years old and he was tested for food sensitivities. He was sensitive to almost his entire diet. At first I couldn't understand why I hadn't seen any signs like a rash or something. Later I discovered I hadn't known what to look for and unlike allergies, food sensitivities do not show up as outer physical signs, but affect the body and brain neurologically.

We moved to Connecticut when Dan was four and Amy was two. They were so unruly, we knew we would never survive a car trip with them out to Connecticut. The company my husband Greg worked for agreed to fly them out and a friend offered to help me with them on the plane.

The three-and-a-half years we spent in Connecticut were tough because we had moved away from the support system of our extended families. Dan became increasingly more mischievous as the years rolled by. As a preschooler he thought it was great fun to lock me out of the house.

One day while we were still living in Connecticut, he ran into the house ahead of me. As I was heading towards the door, I heard a loud crash as something broke. I ran upstairs and found bathtub tiles in the tub along with the soap dish. This was the fifth catastrophe of his day. When I asked him what had happened, he said he was pretending to be Superman and had been walking on the ledge of the building (the edge of the tub.) When he leaped to the soap dish it came off the wall, along with the tiles. He was shocked, but I thought the whole thing was rather humorous until the day I tried to put the soap dish back on the wall and it fell off and broke.

Dan seemed to have an uncanny ability to find things I had hidden. I'll never forget hiding the scissors in the attic after he 'chopped' his sister's hair. He found them about an hour later as if he had seen me hide them. When he was fourteen, he repeated a similar pattern. I had told him he could not ride his sister's bike and I hid the key to her bike lock in the kitchen under a jar of coins. All he needed to do was ask where the key was. As soon as I had pictured in my mind where it was, he immediately went into the house and found it. I am not the only person who has experienced something like this. I know of a therapist who was working with a girl with autism who seemed able to do the same thing. The girl had no verbal skills; during therapy her therapist would say a word and the girl would type it into a computer. One time the therapist only thought the word and before she could say it, the girl had typed it.

We moved back to Minnesota, where Dan started second grade. I enrolled him in public school for second and third grade and sadly watched his love of learning begin to fade. By fourth grade, Dan was unwilling to attend his gifted and talented class because there was only more writing and reading for him to do. I felt their attitude was, 'Oh you're smart, so here's more work for you to do.' This seems to be the general approach for most gifted and talented programs.

Dan started lying about things he had done, which was not like him. In his fourth grade year, he said, 'I hate my life, I want to die.' When I questioned him further, he acted as if he was twenty-five years old, and I hadn't given him a life. He wanted to have a job, build a home of his own, and drive a car. He was so emotionally disturbed over this that I pulled him out of school, and told him, 'You don't have to read or write, just try to be happy.' He said, 'Mom, you're the only one who understands me.' For the most part, that was true. Soon, Dan got a job walking a dog. He designed a fort seven feet off the ground, with real doors and windows, and my brother-in-law built it for him. He sat next to me and learned to drive a car.

By this time, I knew about food sensitivities vs. food allergies. In Dr. Sherry Rogers book, *Depression, Cured At Last* she states, "Food allergy is one of the least diagnosed and one of the most prevalent causes of symptoms, especially depression." We began to take one school year at a time. Dan homeschooled in the fourth and fifth grade.

There had been radon leaking into our house for the three and a half years we had lived in Connecticut. This resulted in Dan having toxins deep in his tissues. We were able to cleanse his system of these toxins and are continuing to manage his mental health concerns naturally. Vitamin D and light therapy improve his Seasonal Affective Disorder (SAD) and a moderately healthy diet keeps him on an even keel.

Dan had a brush with the juvenile system during his early teens and learned about community service and paying fines out of his own hard earned money. He continues to learn things by doing, which is not very safe in this day and age. He began attending a private Christian school in seventh grade, but had to change schools in eighth grade. Dan entered his second Christian school on probation, and God has been working overtime in order to keep him there. He is able to eat 'teenage garbage food,' but he still needs to stay away from artificial colors and sweeteners. Too much soda pop makes him irritable and too many dairy products make him sluggish. They affect his immune system, causing liver problems, which results in acne. Seeing that the liver is responsible for over five hundred bodily functions I feel it is important to teach parents and children what they can do to have a healthy liver. Dan has found 'good' friends which tells me he feels good about himself. He enjoys writing poetry and gave me permission to include some of his work."

Life

Though I have been asked what life means to me,
All I can say is that I'm unsure.
Some people say that it is full of glee,
One thing I know is that we should be pure.
I've been told that life is like a flower,
It starts out young and slowly starts dying.
Some people's only goal in life is power,
Other's lives are so bad that they can't stop crying.
Some say that life is totally unfair,
Others think faith in God will fill all needs.
I've met people who say that they don't care,
Some think life is about doing good deeds.
Life is short, so live for today,
And when life gets hard,
Just sit down and pray.

Dan Vettrus

Dan has always had a great sense of humor. I've included my favorite quote, which he came up with when he was fourteen years old.

"It's the nineties,
You don't stop to smell the roses,
You get one to go!"

Chapter Three

Mary Topero shares her story in order to give hope to parent's who have chosen to medicate or felt they had to medicate their child.

"When I look back, I wonder how I survived it all. As a new family, my husband Bill and I were enjoying our two young sons. One day, Bill said to me, "I think two children is going to be all we need." I responded with, "Three will have to be just right." I had just found out I was pregnant with our third child, Steven. As I write this, I realize how monumental Steven's existence is. If he had never been born, this book most likely would never have been written. Steven was my reason for connecting with Linda Vettrus and co-founding Empowering Parents of Challenging Children, now known as the Whole Child Institute. I am most grateful to him for this, although parenting him to this point has been a huge challenge!

My pregnancy with Steven was quite typical. However, when Steven was born he was somewhat blue due to a lack of oxygen because the cord had been wrapped around his neck. Our healthcare providers sent Steven home from the hospital with no cautions or concerns for us. Steven followed suit with his brothers and was a terrific baby.

It wasn't until he could move about that we knew we had our hands full. Like his older brother Eric, Steven became an overactive toddler and preschooler. He refused to come when he was called and it took drastic measures to get through to him that adults were in charge. He has challenged adult authority his whole life.

At three years, three months Steven was diagnosed with a severe language delay. He used about twenty intelligible words and would act out things he couldn't express verbally.

Sometimes he would hit adult neighbors and even urinate on other children outside.

There were many adjectives which described our blonde, blue eyed toddler and preschooler. Here are just a few—fast, loud, demanding, curious, aggressive, daring, angry, manipulative, stubborn, hyperactive, unpredictable, impulsive, challenging, and somehow, cute-as-a-button. Unfortunately, Steven suffered from many ear infections and was always prescribed antibiotics as a remedy. Eventually, he had tubes placed in his ears and had surgery several times. Over the years, along with all the other challenges we faced with Steven, his ears have continued to be a problem.

As my husband and I searched for help in managing our son, we endured the usual responses from professionals that so many frustrated parents hear. They would say, 'The problem is your parenting ability.' 'Your marriage needs help.' 'It's not the child who has a problem, it's you, the parents' and so on. I often challenged this statement by saying, 'If we are bad parents, why are we only having problems with one out of three children?'

When Steven was three a psychiatrist prescribed antihistamines for him. She reasoned that they would put her to sleep so they should work for Steven and she suggested we try them for a week. What a joke that turned out to be! They didn't phase Steven at all and when we returned, she sent us on our way admitting she couldn't help us. What we hadn't realized at the time is that Steven was dealing with malabsorbtion. His body, rathering than absorbing medication of nutritional supplements was actually dumping them out of his body. We can now understand why he did not react to various medications and the ones that did help always needed to be given in higher and higher doses.

Travelling and so called, 'vacations' were an absolute nightmare. On one trip we even resorted to placing handcuffs on six year old Steven to limit his dangerous movements in the car. It was actually helpful, but we almost ended up in jail when our neighbors heard Steven's version of the story. They alerted the police and before we knew what had happened the police were at our door wanting verification of the story. They requested a chat alone with Steven on the doorstep and about ten minutes later they told us they understood why we had handcuffed Steven, but suggested we find other ways to control him in the future.

At one point, while we were still living in California, I called a mental health agency and told them I was afraid that if I didn't get some *help*, I might hurt my child. They called Child Protection who arrived at our house that very afternoon just as we were getting home from work. Right in front of our children they informed us that they would take our children away from us if we touched them. I called someone asking for *help* and this is what I got? Some help!!

When Steven was evaluated at five he was labeled Temperamental. According to his scores he was pretty severe, exhibiting thirty-eight out of the possible forty characteristics. We were advised to make very strict boundaries and be very consistent. Although we had been doing that Steven's constant bedwetting, severe temper tantrums, hyperactivity and sibling rivalry continued to wear us out.

We moved from Southern California to Minnesota in August of 1988 just before Steven started first grade. He had attended a full-day kindergarten at a Christian School which had been a challenge for both Steven and his teacher, so we didn't waste any time making sure his first grade teacher had fair warning. We told her up front that she was in for a year of challenges with our 'darling' son. I remember so well her comment, 'Don't worry. I've had difficult children in my room before and we'll do just fine.' That positive attitude of hers is what made first grade such a terrific year in school for Steven. However, it didn't take long for the novelty of Steven's new situation to wear off, and the challenge of routine to set in. He was having such significant challenges that by his first conference in the fall I was asked to sign papers for a special education evaluation. Being a trained special education teacher myself, this request came as no surprise. I realize now, that I should have initiated a special education evaluation when Steven was a preschooler.

Steven barely qualified for special services, but the special education teacher managed to squeak him in. It's a good thing she did, because his behavior went from bad to worse. By the middle of second grade he was temporarily placed in an off-site Level 5 EBD program, which is a program for kids whose behavior is so difficult it is not appropriate for them to be in a mainstream classroom. About the same time, Steven had been evaluated by a psychologist who handed us a two-page report on him. Armed with this, we went to see our family practitioner. I said, "Either put this kid on medication or put me on it." It was decided that Steven would be the one taking medication.

At age seven Steven was started on 5 milligrams of Ritalin, but there was so little change, the dosage was increased to 10 mgs. Again, there was not much difference in his behavior. It wasn't until he was taking 15 mgs daily that we could really see a difference in him. Our doctor was not comfortable with such a high dose and he sent us to Minneapolis Children's Hospital for a full evaluation. There it was determined that Steven was dealing with ADHD and should continue on the Ritalin. It was also suggested that the family attend therapy sessions. Boy, was that a fiasco! The five of us, crowded into a small counseling room. Two of our boys were hyperactive. Our eldest son wanted to be the third parent. Honestly, those sessions and the trips home were more hell than life without therapy.

By third grade Steven had improved significantly with a small class size, intensive work, and medication. By the second half of his third grade year Steven was phased back into a mainstream classroom. Soon, however, Steven quickly 'fell off the deep end' and was placed in a Level 4 EBD setting. Then, between the third and fourth grades Steven developed facial twitches and other signs that signified a problem with his medication. After three years on Ritalin it was determined he was intolerant of it, and it was discontinued.

The next three years were agonizing. We tried an array of medications with Steven, including Clonodine, Dexedrine and

Lithium. They either had no effects or caused his behavior to become worse. When we contacted the Head of the Department of Child Psychiatry at the University of Minnesota, he added a new label to Steven's diagnosis, determining that Oppositional Defiant Disorder was now his primary disability. He prescribed Wellbutrin, which was unsuccessful, and finally Cylert. The Cylert helped for attention problems in school, but had no other significant benefits. At this point we felt that we had exhausted all medical avenues. Under a doctors supervision, we slowly took Steven off his medication in May of 1994 and decided to search for more healthy means of dealing with his problems.

When Steven was ten, we took him to Dr. Crocker at Allergy Associates in La Crosse, Wisconsin. There we discovered that he was highly allergic to eggs and dairy products. We also found that hypoglycemia was a problem, thus sugary treats for rewards were damaging rather than helpful. He was also allergic to air-borne allergens such as mold, dust, yeast and pollens. Using the principles of homeopathy, "like cures like," Dr. Crocker prescribed drops of antigens. These were administered sublingually (under the tongue). We eliminated eggs, cheeses, butter, and sugar from Steven's diet. This upset him, but we did notice some immediate improvement including a decrease in aggressive behavior and the frequency of colds.

By May of 1995 we were still unable to find help that would really make a significant and long lasting difference. We had tried public school with special education and mainstreaming, an expensive private school, homeschooling, and a combination with home and school, but life was still very challenging.

I attended a Touch for Health class and learned about a bioflavanoid food supplement. Four months after Steven had been literally saturated with this substance, we could honestly say he had greatly improved. The school staff had nothing but positive comments to report to us.

As a family, we enjoyed a happier disposition in our daily lives and interaction with one another. Steven was more balanced emotionally and was capable of following directions, staying on task, and being more responsible/accountable for his behavior. He became aware of and accepted his allergies and food sensitivities taking responsibility for his body and how he felt physically. Also, since Steven began a nutritional regimen the health of his ears was better and his hearing returned to normal.

Steven took a nose dive at age fifteen and began eating junk food where he worked. He became extremely oppositional as he fought to be a young adult. At one point we needed to sign a form which gave us the right to his pay checks. This tactic worked quite well in order to help Steven realize who was boss. I called for back up and created a children's mental health wrap around for him. I hired a tutor and included her in the wrap around team. Steven at this point was attending high school half time and being home schooled half time. Other members of the team included a psychologist, psycho therapist/child advocate, a family friend, and neighbor. Steven's wrap around meetings were held monthly. We began to see Steven slowly change and it became obvious to all that I needed to let go and let him suffer his own consequences.

Steven has now set goals for himself including attending vocational college to learn more about small engines and hopefully open his own machine shop with his brother Eric.

I attribute Steven's great success in life at this point to a combination of programs. The Minneapolis Children's Mental Health Wrap Around, the karate program he attended (primarily for young children dealing with ADHD), and the three years of in-home personal care attendants provided by Medical Assistance (TEFRA). These people helped us deal more effectively with Steven and kept him at home where he could learn how to function around his family. There were recreational and adaptive recreational programs and camps. There were also a number of caring professionals: The great doctors at Allergy Associates in Wisconsin, chiropractors, many coaches and assistants in the various sports he has played, scouting and dedicated volunteer leaders, as well as Touch for

Health and Kinetic Education instructors. There were many wonderful books and publications I used for information and guidance which I've listed in the resource section of this book. There were organizations like ChADD (Children and Adults with Attention Deficit Disorder), PACER Center (Parent Advocacy Coalition for Educational Rights), LDM (Learning Disabilities of Minnesota, MACMH (Minnesota Association for Children's Mental Health), the Minnesota Bio-Brain Association, Twin Cities Autism Society, Family and Children's Services, MN Children Families & Learning (formerly the MN Department of Education), the natural food and supplement industries, as well as many dedicated and loving individuals who supported us in our desperate search for answers.

I am excited that now we have a son who we are very proud of and who is much more able to control his behavior. The Richfield, Minnesota school District is to be commended for all their diligence and support of Steven and our family. I hope my family's success will inspire many other parents and professionals to reach out and learn more natural ways of dealing with families in crisis."

The following document was written for professionals, especially teachers, who come into contact with Steven. After sitting through meetings where only Steven's negative side was talked about, Mary Topero felt that this document would be helpful in order to get meetings off to a positive start. Strengths and assets are purposely listed before needs and weaknesses. Mary encourages parents to follow suit and write a similar overview of their child.

STEVEN TOPERO
A Brief Overview by Parents

MOST PERTINENT HISTORY

- Lack of oxygen, blue at birth, third child (2 older brothers both graduated from Richfield High School, Richfield, MN.)
- Lots of ear infections, antibiotics, tubes in ears several times.
- Very challenging behavior (linked to inability to express himself verbally.)
- Diagnosed *severe language delayed* at age 3 years. 3 months.
- Diagnosed *"temperamental"* at age 5 by a clinical psychologist (in California.)
- Moved only once—California to Richfield, MN summer l988 (just before first grade.)
- Diagnosed w/ Attention Deficit Hyperactivity Disorder at age 7 (Children's Hospital)
- Diagnosed with allergies in 5th grade—eggs, dairy, dust, mold, yeast, pollens, magic markers.
- Diagnosed Hypoglycemic in 6th grade (sugar consumption directly affected behavior.)
- Diagnosed severely delayed in Visual Integration Processing—therapy followed, 7th gr.
- Oppositional Defiant Disorder—primary diagnosis at about age eleven.
- TYMPANOPLATOMY—ear surgery, Feb. of 8th grade.
- Ninth grade—being assessed for Auditory Integration Processing difficulties.
- Steven and family have been through years of counseling, assessments, therapies, etc.

STRENGTHS / ASSESTS

- Persistent, works hard at what he is **interested** in and **motivated** to do.
- Discovered he liked art and showed some talent starting in 8th grade.
- Loves small engines: strong mechanical aptitude—talks about having his own business.
- Has participated in group sports: baseball (favorite), soccer, basketball, and football.
- Enjoys target shooting, reading the newspaper (sports page), Nintendo, solitaire on the computer, and casual ball playing.
- Performs well individually and in small groups—good discussion group participant.
- Lovable, affectionate, loves back scratches—likes body brush and massage.
- Money motivated, has had jobs since age 8: prompt, dependable, independent; does not ask parents for money—bought own clothes and school supplies for 9th grade.
- Very good with little children, has worked with neighbor's grandchildren and with children at the YMCA.
- Participated in Y Start program in 7th and 8th grade and benefited from it.
- Really into body building—lifting weights, swimming (w/ ear plugs), working out at YMCA and is responsible to pay for his own membership dues monthly.
- Has his own checkbook and is using it to learn money management and responsibility.
- Interested in wrestling, boxing, has earned 4 belts in Karate and paid for half of his lessons himself.
- Motivated by need for a B average in order to drive when parents feel he is ready and mature enough to handle the responsibility and judgement calls.
- Two parents—who give lots of family support, advocacy, encouragement, guidelines, and tough love.
- Learning self-advocacy skills.

- Has developed "emotional intelligence" by resisting eating eggs and dairy—sugar is harder to resist, but his "body/brain connection" is improving.
- Has been on 6 different kinds of medications, has gone through major detoxification and is on natural substances (medication free for over 2 years.)
- Abides by curfew and generally remembers to call home about change in plans, etc.
- Has participated in Boy Scouts for many years and is working on rank of Star, is developing many good leadership skills, and loves the activities and camping events.

NEEDS / WEAKNESSES

- Responds well to fresh air and water when his allergies act up (red ears, puffiness under the eyes, increase in oppositional and inappropriate behaviors.
- Needs intake of fresh air frequently during school day.
- In class, needs to sit up front and to teacher's right when facing the class (right ear tends to stay healthiest.)
- Needs to sit in the front of the bus: prevents behavior problems—less intake of exhaust.
- Hearing is affected by frequent colds—sometimes hard to tell if he is listening or having problems hearing.
- Diet directly affects health and emotional stability—**NO SUGAR REWARDS**.
- Needs immediate help with conflict resolution—very limited problem solving skills.
- **Needs help with social skills**—keeping friends and making healthy friendships.
- In the past he has had difficulty respecting authority.
- Mother/son relationship is stressed—responds well to father and other males.

- Lacks cooperation for chores at home—short fuse, needs quick jobs that are simple and do not require organizational skills.
- Difficulty being successful in large groups—often times over-stimulating.
- Difficult to divert his desire to watch violence or inappropriate entertainment.
- Needs immediate as well as short term consequences—both negative and positive.
- Easily distracted and has difficulty staying on task—especially a difficult task.
- Has a long history of difficulty following directions; reponds best to as few directions as possible.
- Needs a note taker and/or assistance with written assignments (major frustration.)
- The more he writes the sloppier he tends to get, this fine motor task involves much emotion.
- In general, school has not been a positive experience.
- Transitions are difficult—monitoring sometimes necessary.
- Difficulty with eating choices in cafeteria—needs healthy alternative to dairy.
- Short lunch breaks are challenging for him.

EXPECTATIONS FOR STEVEN

- That he do his best, think about one class and one day at a time (work on not being overwhelmed.)
- Work on organizational skills, following directions, respect, being where he belongs, social skills, making smart choices, being accountable for his actions, caring for personal and school property, following the rules and guidelines.
- Work on time management in relation to school assignments.

EXPECTATIONS OF STAFF

- Say to Steven, "Do your BEST" rather than "TRY!" or "You can do it."
- Help Steven to achieve his expectations.
- Communicate with parents immediately for any conflict resolution that needs parental reinforcement.
- Whenever possible encourage water drinking and taking fresh air breaks.
- Due to his high need for water, frequent bathroom passes may be necessary.

Chapter Four

Keith's story is a classic example of how important early intervention can be. Keith was a very toxic child. As a toddler his parents unknowingly exposed him to lead-based mini-blinds which he played with. Toxins from his asthma medication had also built up in his system and a clinical nutritionist noted that the insides of his intestines were probably similar to raw meat. Chiropractic adjustments only released these toxins, making his behavior almost intolerable one to two days after an adjustment. Keith received the most help from a liquid detoxification protocol prescribed by the clinical nutritionist. His mother used many resources to help Keith. Perhaps you can relate to her story.

"I had a very good pregnancy with Keith, and he was an incredible infant. He was extremely easy to care for and slept through the night early on. He was a busy baby, had a great appetite, and hardly ever cried. He moved around early and cut his first tooth at five months. He stopped nursing at three months and was independent rather quickly. He wasn't much of a sit down-and-relax kind of kid, and he didn't like to cuddle. It was probably when he reached about fifteen months of age that he learned how to open up 'childproof ' locks and would climb up on things.

My husband and I were concerned about this early activity and when we approached our doctor she felt he fit into the Active/Alert category. We hadn't considered him to be hyperactive so we felt that Active/Alert described Keith rather well. He was diagnosed with asthma in October of 1994, just before his second birthday and was put on Albuterol and Intol. His behavior became worse, but we didn't realize that it was due to the medications he was being given. A few weeks later a parent from his daycare, who happened to be a pharmacist, noticed how hyper and uncooperative Keith was getting and suggested the medication he was on may be causing the increase in his negative behavior. That's when we found out that Albuterol is almost pure caffeine.

At three years old, Keith was not sleeping through the night, very hyperactive, and driving everybody 'wacko.' He wasn't getting along well at daycare, he was in trouble a lot, and bothering the other kids. I was concerned because he was gradually becoming uncontrollable.

I started researching what the label Active/Alert meant and shortly afterwards found out about a natural food supplement that might help. I started him on that for his asthma and was able to gradually take him off the Albuterol and Intol. He has been completely free of those drugs since December of 1995.

My husband and I learned about the Whole Child Institute at a business meeting for a multi-level marketing company that is concerned with nutrition and distributes the natural food supplement I had discovered. One of the speakers that evening had mentioned the Whole Child Institute so we spoke with a representative afterwards. We decided to have Keith assessed. He came through the assessment very well, although it was noted that he was on and off his chair a lot. As my husband and I observed him during his assessment, we began to see how hyperactive he really was and this confirmed what I had been suspecting even after taking him off his asthma medication; he was probably dealing with ADHD. This gave me a starting point to work with and I began doing some research. I attended a class on ADD/ADHD given by John Taylor, Ph.D. He also confirmed my feelings that Keith was dealing with ADHD and gave me some ideas how I could help him.

Through the Whole Child Institute we learned about alternative resources that would help Keith. Using natural supplements and making some dietary changes, made it possible for Keith to sleep through the night.

The dietary changes we made helped his attitude and temperament. At first, his daycare provider wasn't comfortable with us changing his foods because she was concerned it would be too hard on him not being able to have what the rest of the kids had. We switched him from whole or 2% milk to 1% or skim milk, which he took to very well. Under the direction of a doctor we eventually switched him to a non-dairy substitute. We use it in baking and on his cereal, but we've used good pure water as a beverage. We encourage liquids between meals in order to allow for a healthier breakdown of his foods. He actually did the whole food switch over very well and without any problems at all. He seemed like a whole different child in the sense that he would actually slow down, stop, listen to us, and process what we were saying to him.

We withdrew Keith from his daycare setting and enrolled him in the pilot program at the Whole Child Institute. The first day Keith had exhausted his primary staff person by 10:00 a.m. She began to suspect that Keith might be headed toward diabetes, which was later confirmed by a doctor of preventative medicine. He was still on some dairy and his first morning at the Whole Child Institute we sent some skim milk and cold cereal sweetened with refined sugar, for his breakfast. We were told we might want to consider taking sugar out of his diet. One of the reasons we were given was his high activity level, but another reason was that he would go to the bathroom so much. He wouldn't drink that much, but he would go so many times, which is a symptom of diabetes.

We didn't give him any kind of sugar the rest of that day or the next morning and he didn't wear out his primary staff member until noon. He had no sugar or dairy over the weekend, and he did great the following Monday until that afternoon when he was taken to the grocery store. When the staff member stopped to talk with someone, he grabbed the cart and tried yanking her down the aisle. She was pretty worn out by the time they left the store. Since most toxins in our environment reside close to the floor, at a child's level, he was probably affected by the toxins in the grocery store and suddenly became very hyper.

Whole Child Institute

The first thing Keith experienced at the Whole Child Institute was a hand holding technique developed by co-founder Linda Vettrus especially for him. She would take him by the hand when he came in the door, walk him to a chair, and have him sit down. He couldn't get up until he told her what he wanted to do. They would discuss what he was going to do next and why he wanted to get down from his chair. This lengthened the time that he could actually sit in one spot, and it also helped with his impulsivity and his lack of obedience.

We started seeing positive changes in his behavior, so we knew we were on to something with the Whole Child Institute. When I used to pick him up from daycare, he would have a temper tantrum. He'd yell and scream and have fits. When I picked him up at the Whole Child Institute, we were taught how to handle even this exhausting behavior. As he threw a fit while we were leaving he was told that if he was going to act like that he would be taken back inside. He would cry and say he wanted his mom and finally would 'melt' and shape up. He would then be able to come back out to me. One day I picked him up and he managed to get outside OK, but then he wanted to get to our van. I was still talking to a staff member and he started pulling me by the hand over and over. I finally let go and he fell onto the ground. He got back up and started pulling again. I let go, and once again he fell to the ground. It took him a while to learn that he couldn't do that. Now, he can make those types of transitions in one collected piece and at times not even talk back to me. It has just been a wonderful change to see because it's something we really worked hard at.

Through the Whole Child Institute, we learned about the dietary changes we could make. We were introduced to resource people who understood what we were going through and what Keith was really dealing with. We now understand Keith's learning styles and have put into practice parenting techniques which help us deal with him. Sometimes we just ignore Keith's behaviors and don't respond. He likes to get into debates, and I might go back and forth with him a couple of times and then I'll tell him it's the end of the discussion and I ignore all other comments. He'll usually just drop it then. Sometimes I just go along with it and then he'll change his mind and do exactly what I want him to do. Here's one example: I'll say, 'Keith it's time to take a bath. We've got to get you in the tub, it's bath night." He'll say, "No. I don't want to take a bath.' I respond with, 'Well, you need to. You won't have a bath until the day after tomorrow, and you need to get clean.' He'll say, 'No, I don't want to.' So I just say, 'OK, well then, don't take a. bath.' And he finally says, 'OK Mom, I'll take a bath.'

Right now Keith is detoxifying. His body is gradually getting rid of the toxins that have built up over the years, such as medications, lead and cadmium. His present challenges are disobedience and talking back to me. He has a hard time obeying authority and he continually challenges me physically and verbally. My husband and I realize that part of this is our parenting, since we are so busy we don't always follow through. He doesn't have a lot of consistency at home and he doesn't always know what his boundaries are because we aren't as clear about them as we should be. With help from the Whole Child Institute we improved our parenting skills and witnessed daily improvements.

We have heard remarks from friends and family about the positive changes in Keith since we improved his diet and started him on natural supplements. It is encouraging when they say they can see him improving. Sometimes when you live with it everyday, you don't always notice the changes. Just about everyone in both of our families has noted that they have seen many positive changes in him since we began working with the Whole Child Institute."

As Keith's mother stated, "He doesn't have consistency at home and he doesn't always know what his boundaries are." This created some parent-inflicted ADHD (Attention Deficit Hyperactivity Disorder). He was allowed to wander through the house doing "his own thing." Structured activities, schedules, and organization were not always a part of his home environment. Keith's parents have been diligent in working to help their son overcome his behavioral challenges. Their hard work has really paid off. He is in a mainstream kindergarten and his teacher's only complaint at the beginning of the school year was that he talked out of turn. She immediately placed a call to his parents and the situation was remedied. At that point, just knowing that his teacher was teamed up with his parents did the trick for Keith. Wow, what a change!

"Children have more need of models than of critics."

—*Carolyn Coats*

Chapter Five

Tommy's mother was at her "wit's end" when she brought him to the Whole Child Institute. Tommy struggled with sensory integration processing. He was unable to accurately process what he received through his various senses (smell, taste, sight, hearing and touch). Her story relates the frustration and paranoia parents often feel when dealing with children who are challenging.

"Tommy was our first child. I think with your first child, you don't really know what's going on. You certainly don't have anyone to compare their behavior to. I did admit, however, that compared to other children he was different, but he exhibited nothing that concerned me enough to take him to a doctor.

We didn't put him in a preschool program until he was four because he just didn't seem ready for it. The program for three-year olds seemed developmentally more appropriate for him, so we enrolled him in that one. After about six weeks, the teachers told us that Tommy was having a lot of problems. He didn't know how to keep himself occupied. His worst times were during unstructured playtime. Although he liked to look at books, he had no idea how to relate to people, especially children his own age. He wouldn't keep his hands to himself and he couldn't stay on task. At first, we didn't take this news very well and we thought they were finding things that didn't exist.

As Tommy approached five, we were notified that in Minnesota parents are required to have Early Childhood testing done the year before their child enters kindergarten. Even though we weren't planning on sending him to kindergarten as a five year old, we had him tested. That's when an occupational therapist discovered that he didn't know how to hold a crayon much less color with it. I am an artist, and although I had encouraged him, I always thought he just didn't want to do it. I didn't know that kids are naturally interested in coloring. He was tested further and qualified for Early Childhood Special Education at his school.

He enjoyed the Early Childhood Special Ed Program, although I wasn't sure if it was the right place for him. A parent support group was offered during his class time so I took advantage of the opportunity to gain some understanding and help for myself.

At my first meeting, as I was describing my son's problems, a woman said, "It sounds like he could really use the help of my daughter's occupational therapist. Why don't you give her a call?" I took her up on the idea. Tommy did not have an official diagnosis, but his symptoms were severe enough in the area of sensory integration processing that the occupational therapist agreed to see him and work with him. He then started an occupational therapy program that lasted eleven months.

At first Tommy went three times a week and then just twice weekly. He would start out with gross motor activities that had a calming effect on him. This included sit-bouncing on a big ball, crawling through a tunnel, and using a special swing. He would swing on his stomach while pulling on a strap which controlled his swinging motions. Apparently, that kind of motion was very soothing and very good for his nervous system. My husband eventually made a swing like that for Tommy because he loved it so much. His Occupational Therapist was able to coax him into a whirlpool, which is where Tommy first put his head under water. This was a huge victory even though, so far, he hasn't done that for me! To develop fine motor skills, she had him work on puzzles, play memory games, and search for objects hidden in big tubs full of beads or sand.

We supplemented the program at home by brushing his skin with a surgical scrub brush. We were instructed to run the brush up and down his back, legs, and arms with just enough pressure to bend the bristles. The frequency of this activity was gradually decreased as the program continued. His therapist showed us how to compress his joints at the shoulders, elbows, wrists, knees, and ankles. This was very important for improving his body/ brain connections and had a noticeable calming affect on him.

Occupational therapy helped us a lot. His therapist was wonderful and Tommy made a great deal of progress during his sessions with her. The most important thing that came out of that whole program was his ability to withstand sensations on his skin. He was eventually able to tolerate having a damp washcloth used on his face and having his hair washed without screaming. In terms of sensory integration, he could tolerate a greater variety of textures of clothing and was somewhat able to handle having his hair brushed. He started to understand the difference between left and right as well as develop a concept of time. Apparently, all these things are inter-linked and if they don't fall into place by the time a child is three this type of therapy for sensory integration processing can help them along. Tommy began to get a sense of internal organization that he had previously lacked. It made such a big difference in his life, and we were so impressed. We thought, "Well this is it; this is the answer." Once we get done with this sensory integration therapy, then he'll be OK."

Well, we soon found out that no *one* thing is ever the answer. After a while, all the results from the brushing and occupational therapy reached a plateau. Even though Tommy was much better in many ways, his reactions to different environments were still very unpredictable.

As a parent of a child like this, you gradually adapt your life to the child's behavior. Without realizing it you structure the environment in order to minimize his reactions and end up completely planning your day around one child. Due to unpredictable and sometimes embarrassing behavior you begin taking him into risky environments less and less, and you become isolated.

That summer Tommy attended his Special Education Program and participated in occupational therapy to further develop his fine motor skills. Instead of going to kindergarten in the fall as a five year old he did another year of Early Childhood Special Education which concentrated on his fine and gross motor skills.

The following summer I found myself at my wit's end with his behavior. His emotional outbursts had become worse. We soon learned about perseveration, a word which explained so much of his behavior. For example, one day he brought a small plastic toy to me and said, 'Mom!, Mom!, I want to make a hundred of these, I want to make a 1000 of these, I want 25 to be blue, and I want 25 to be green; I want 25 to be white, and I want 25 to be black.......' 'Mom, how do you make these?' He would have long ramblings like this and then just walk away. Minutes later he'd be back and start the whole thing over again. That's what the month of July was like that summer. He was so immersed in his own world. When he begged me for information, it was as if he was unable to process my responses and we would have to go over and over it. I felt like tearing my hair out!

One night my husband and I were so confused and frustrated with him that we actually prayed together to be guided to a solution. The next morning I found a brochure for the Whole Child Institute at a health food store. I thought, 'Oh, maybe I should give them a call; what's it going to hurt?' My only alternative was calling my friend who is a child psychologist and to have invited her over to observe Tommy at home. From her observations I probably would have been advised to consider medication. I just didn't know what to do anymore.

I contacted the Whole Child Institute and was able to get a whole child assessment within a few days. Up to this point I had considered myself well read and well educated. I was very careful to buy whole wheat bread, peanut butter with no sugar, jam with no refined sugar, etc. Although I didn't buy organic fruits and vegetables on a regular basis, I would sometimes shop at a health food store. I felt I was doing enough and I considered myself a very educated food consumer. By way of the whole child assessment I was able to see that Tommy might have a sensitivity to wheat, potatoes, peas, corn products, refined sugar, dairy products…, even fruits. I thought, 'What?' 'How can this be?' We were told later by a clinical nutritionist that Tommy was dealing with too much Vitamin B and it was suggested that we cut the wheat bread out of his diet for awhile.

I started eliminating these particular foods from his diet. I also started giving him some food supplements. These were given in order to help balance his blood sugar and to help his body and brain detoxify so nutrients could be absorbed. I also gave him zinc, a flax preparation, mineral supplements, and garlic if he got sick. Before I knew it I had this child that looked the same, but did not act like the same child at all! I couldn't believe it! As a result of what I learned at the assessment, I felt empowered to help myself as well as my child. I changed his diet the week before school began, which is never a good time to start anything new, but we had to do something fast. I went to his school and told his teachers about the foods we were eliminating from his diet. I told them he was not to drink milk or eat their crackers and that I would supply his snack. The staff was skeptical but I stood firm because I had seen such a big change in just the first week of avoiding foods he was sensitive to.

Four weeks later he begged me for some dried apricots, which was one of his favorite treats. I told him, 'That's really not on your list of things to eat.' He begged and begged and I finally let him have some. A few hours later he ended up with terrible diarrhea. He looked at me and said, 'Is this because I ate apricots?' and I said, 'I think so.' That episode is significant because he never had made connections like that before. An awareness of cause and effect had not previously existed for him. It was astounding to his father and I. It still is!

Going to the grocery store with this child was something I either tried to avoid or tried to do early in the day. It seemed that the later in the day I went shopping, the worse time we would have. I wouldn't go if it was past four o'clock in the afternoon. This is another example of how I felt my life was controlled by Tommy's behavior.

One day, I found I *had* to go to the grocery store. It was five o'clock and I thought, 'I'm just going to have to do it.' We got to the produce section and he asked for a piece of fruit, which he wasn't supposed to have, so I said, 'No.' And all he said was, 'OK Mommy,' instead of fighting and having a big fit. I cannot explain the momentousness of this event. I looked at him in shock and I couldn't even think of what to say. We kept walking down the produce aisle and this was repeated a couple of times until we got down to the end of the aisle and he said, 'Look Mommy, my brain says I can be good now. You can tell me 'No' and I don't have to cry.' I thought, 'What has happened to this kid?' I was just floored. I couldn't believe it! He told me, 'My heart and my brain are telling me, 'Be good Tommy.''

It was like having a glimpse into what normal life with my child could be. I was convinced at this point that the changes were directly related to his new dietary regime and the food supplements he was taking.

Over the course of the next few months we saw other evidences of improvement. Tommy became interested in artwork, he behaved well at the dentist's office, and he started Kumon Math. When it came to structured learning he used to be emotionally and mentally shut down, but Tommy had also participated in the Whole Child Institute's Learning Gap Therapy Program, which helped to increase his body/brain connections and prepared him to participate in the Kumon Math program.

Tommy was five months into his dietary changes and had been attending the Kumon Center for four months when he got into some candy and gum one hour before working on his Kumon Math worksheets. *It normally would have taken him about ten minutes to complete his work with no errors.* On this particular day it took him twenty-seven minutes, not to mention twenty-eight errors by the time he had finished. His errors began on the very first page and continued to multiply. The sugar had really kicked in by the next day and he got fifty-two wrong in fifty minutes. On the third day the effects of the sugar were still apparent; his score was forty-three wrong in thirty-nine minutes. I was shocked that the sugar had affected him for three days. It had taken him so long to complete his work, I was surprised that he had actually finished it. His time of ten minutes per day had been sufficient and normal for his age.

Tommy enjoys the Kumon Program and thinks it's fun. We are excited about the prospect of enrolling him in the Kumon Reading Program because Kumon uniquely addresses the way he learns. His Dad has been supportive participating in learning activities with him and learning about ways that we can help him.

The other thing I did, which was very helpful, was to consult with a homeopathic practitioner. Homeopathy has a seemingly subtle, but I think a very powerful effect. It's done a lot for Tommy as far as calming his fears. I give him a homeopathic remedy for fear and that helps in conjunction with his diet.

Before I started addressing his food sensitivities I would have to renew his remedy every six weeks. Afterwards, I went sixteen weeks without giving him any. I just never saw a need to give it to him because paying attention to his food sensitivities had made such an improvement in our lives. It was amazing!

My husband and I were involved in the alcohol and drug scene as young adults. We strongly suspect we have passed on heavy chemical toxicity to our sons. Our younger son has not been as dramatically affected as Tommy, probably because we had changed to a healthier lifestyle before conceiving him. Yet his immune system was definitely compromised and he frequently suffers from colds and infections. Considering our family history, we are thankful that the Whole Child Institute directed us to see a clinical nutritionist in order to help us remove the chemical toxins from our children's systems.

People are resistant, or better yet skeptical, about my seeking alternative treatments. It all sounds kind of weird to people who are immersed in the 'medical model.' I had the advantage of initially being somewhat on the fringe medically. I personally see an acupuncturist and have always taken my kids to a homeopath. However, at times, even the most determined of us can feel like it's not worth it to pursue alternative methods, feeling like we're fighting an uphill battle all by ourselves. It is very comforting to know that I have people on my side who understand what I am going through. It was important for helping me maintain sanity especially when initially my spouse didn't agree with me, my family didn't agree with me, and none of my friends agreed with what I was trying to do. It's nice to know there are people who have the same concerns about medication and are trying to do different things to help children by taking a 'first do no harm' approach.

At this point we now have a lot of puzzle pieces fitting together. The issues we still face with Tommy are major impulse control and difficulty with change. He also needs to learn interactive play skills. Those three things are still very big hurdles for us to address. All of the things I've learned from the Whole Child Institute—the books they have referred me to, the ideas they have introduced me to, the professionals and products they've suggested, have all had a positive effect on my child. No one thing is a cure for these kids. If I had not come in contact with the Whole Child Institute, Tommy, as a six-year old, would probably be on some kind of medication. I don't know. It's hard to say. I'm extremely thankful that he's doing so well."

Tommy has gone from a child who cried when presented with new learning material to a confident, 'I can do it,' kind of kid. He exhibits socially appropriate behavior and is still working on eye contact. He is a joy to be around.

Chapter Six

Aaron was under house arrest when his mother contacted the Whole Child Institute. He is a very nice young man who was failed by his school system as well as the judicial system. Although his parents did what they could, challenging children tend to burn out their caregivers. When professionals cannot relate to their situation, they react in disbelief. If Aaron's auditory integration processing problem had been addressed early on, along with the Feingold Diet, he may never have ended up in the juvenile court system for his anger outbursts. His mother shares Aaron's incredible journey.

"Aaron, our fifteen year old son, has diagnoses of Obsessive Compulsive Disorder, Depression, and ADHD, as well as an auditory integration processing problem. In the beginning, we did not have names for his problems, but on this long and frustrating road, we discovered them while striving to be advocates for our son.

When Aaron was eight weeks old, he almost slept through the night. As a toddler, it had been very difficult to get him to sleep at night. He would usually fall asleep around midnight or 1:00 AM. Even though he would awaken two to four times during the night, he would be up for the day around 6:30 or 7:00 in the morning. We tried everything we could think of to change this pattern.

By the time Aaron was eighteen months old, he had entirely given up naps; other than occasionally when I would drive around town with him for my own sanity. He could fall asleep in the car but otherwise, he just could not wind down.

Aaron was always ahead of his peers developmentally. He was walking by the time he was nine months old. When I took him in for his fifteen month, well-baby check-up, the doctor was very surprised that Aaron was speaking in full sentences. He informed me that Aaron's speech was at the level of a two - year-old.

Early on Aaron had a lot of emotional and behavioral outbursts. I called them 'grandmal' temper tantrums. He would have a sort of a different look on his face, like he was on another planet, and then go into a rage. Sometimes we could tell what would trigger it. Other times he would wake up from a nap and all of a sudden become belligerent.

We couldn't control him. We tried time outs, but he would not stay on a chair or go into his room. Sometimes, when he would be thrashing and kicking around with a really bad temper tantrum, I would try holding him down by wrapping my legs around his in order to keep both of us safe. He could go into this Jekyll-and-Hyde behavior at seemingly any moment. The flip side of this was that he could be an absolute delight. He was extremely active and bright.

My husband and I were terribly exhausted during these years. When he was three years old, I took him into the doctor for a physical. I described what we were going through. I told the doctor about his sleeping patterns, the temper tantrums, his out of control behavior, the lack of sleep, and all of the things we were doing in order to control his behaviors. The doctor just looked at me and didn't seem to believe what I was telling her.

By this time I had seen a total of eight different doctors in eight different clinics and had been given no help at all. I had talked to most of them about whether or not Aaron was hyperactive. No one seemed to think so. Basically, I was told that he was not hyperactive, but only on the high end of the activity scale. My husband and I went through parenting classes, but no one there seemed to have any advice for us, especially with his 'grand mal' temper tantrums. I would frequently talk to a Special Education teacher, who attended our church, about how to handle him. We were doing our best to learn and to deal with his behavior.

When Aaron was three-and-a-half, I went to a church meeting and a woman said, 'Beth, you look awful!' 'You look really tired!' I broke down into tears and started describing what our life was like with so very little sleep. Someone over hearing me poor my heart out suggested a book by Dr. Ben Feingold entitled, *Why Your Child Is Hyperactive.* I read the book and decided to try the diet. It meant eliminating artificial flavors, artificial colors, and foods that naturally contain salicylates which are chemically similar in structure. These would be almonds, apples, apricots, cherries, currants, all berries, peaches, plums, prunes, tomatoes, cucumbers, and oranges.

Five days after beginning the diet, we had briefly left Aaron in our family room in order to set out the trash for the night. Upon entering the house we found that he had vanished. By 10:00 at night Aaron was usually very wound up so we figured we had our work cut out for us just trying to find him. My husband ran outside and I started checking everywhere around the house. Ironically, the very last place we checked was his room. Aaron had tucked himself into bed and was fast asleep. For the first time in his life, he slept through the entire night. He slept for a solid fourteen hours! The following afternoon, he took a four-and-a-half hour nap. The poor kid had been absolutely exhausted all his life. When my mother saw him, the following week, she said, 'He used to be like a spring waiting to be sprung and sometimes he did.' All of a sudden, Aaron had simply relaxed.

With this diet, we were able to use time-out, we were able to talk to him, and we could use more normal disciplinary tactics. We did not have any of the long term temper tantrums, which ran anywhere from one to three hours. If he pitched a little fit, it would last five or ten minutes and then it was over. He would actually respond positively to the words, 'No,' or 'Go sit down and take a time out.'

The Feingold diet was truly a miracle sent by God! Aaron could sleep through the night and be more reasonable and rational. He was much more of a delight to be around.

We noticed, a few times when he ate something he shouldn't, he wouldn't be able to settle down and sleep. Even certain toothpastes would set him off for seventy-two hours almost to the minute. We had a number of setbacks like this. They would start up within an hour or two of his eating or being exposed to things he was sensitive to. For instance, I discovered that I couldn't give him Amoxicillin for ear infections because of the red dye it contained, and instead used an antibiotic without red dye.

In the early years of school when Aaron was in kindergarten, he was doing fairly well. Behaviorally he had a few ups and downs and sometimes he was a little more withdrawn than the other kids. We were concerned because he didn't want to be in school. If things weren't really exciting to him he didn't want to participate. He would kind of back out of it and sit on the sidelines. Although he was not a major behavior problem in class, he did get frustrated when he didn't understand what was going on academically.

I had told Aaron's second grade teacher to expect a worsening of his behavior in the fall because of his sensitivity to pollens and she didn't believe me. But one day she said he had come in from recess and it was like a light switch. He had been a delight, a hard worker, and cooperative. The next thing she knew he was obnoxious and totally off the wall. He had returned to the classroom after recess, laid down on his desk and proceeded to do swimming motions.

During this time his class was given a national standardized test and Aaron did not do very well. A few weeks later his behavior switched back to normal. I asked that he be tested again, and this time he placed well into the 90th percentile in every subject. This confirmed to me that his allergies and his chemical composition had a great deal to do with his ability to learn and produce work.

After Christmas vacation of his fifth grade year, Aaron had become one of the many 'behavior problems' in his classroom. I tried to get help for him by going through the appropriate channels at the school, but it was a very slow process. Aaron was no longer getting good grades and once again he didn't like going to school. He was having problems with peer relationships, and was involved in many fights.

Between fifth and sixth grade, we took him to the University of Minnesota where he was diagnosed with ADHD. The professionals there told us Aaron should have a Section 504 accommodation plan, which essentially is a plan for teachers to make accommodations for a student's disabilities. He did not qualify for a Special Education Program, but he did have a diagnosis which by law, gave him the right to have an accommodation plan at school. We met with his school staff in order to set up such a plan. Part of Aaron's accommodation plan stated that teachers were to send home written assignments with him so he understood exactly what his assignments were.

Early on in Junior High, Aaron earned a bad reputation with his teachers. He wasn't getting his work in. He didn't know his assignments and the teachers figured they shouldn't have to repeat things for him. I found out that none of them knew of his accommodation plan, although his file had been transferred from the elementary school. I tried to explain that he was dealing with ADHD and that he wasn't always able to process what he heard. We hadn't known about auditory integration processing yet, but I knew that there were times when he heard us, yet wasn't able to process what we were saying. Through the years some of his teachers had not believed him when he said he hadn't understood what they were saying. This had the potential to cause tension between Aaron and his teachers.

It wasn't until he was fifteen that we had an audiologist screen him for a possible auditory integration processing problem. The screening revealed a significant deficit in his auditory processing abilities.

Aaron did try very hard at the beginning of eighth grade. He would get up in the morning, shower, dress, have breakfast, and be out the door in about twenty minutes. As the year progressed, he became traumatized over his poor school performance, the 'wannabe' gang kids, and the multiple fights that took place at school. It was all a very scary and devastating place for him.

From that point on things seemed to go steadily downhill for Aaron. He began to take a long time getting ready for school which was a manifestation of Obsessive Compulsive Disorder. He suffered serious bouts of depression. During one episode he made an unsuccessful attempt at suicide by taking an overdose of an over-the-counter medication. He experimented with drugs and alcohol. He became so violent at home that sometimes we had to call the police. Eventually, he was hospitalized for depression.

Aaron has been shuffled around from school to school and program to program for most of his life. The routine and consistent environment, which is so important for these children, has always eluded him. For the school, it was either a money issue or just that the staff was unwilling to try to understand Aaron and they would hand him off to someone else.

Consistency still seems to be out of reach for Aaron. Recently, we were told he would be out of his current program after attending for only four months! We strongly objected to this, because he is doing so well there and it has taken fifteen years for Aaron to get where he is at; four months time is not enough to get him turned around completely and ready for a mainstream school.

Through The Carl Pfieffer Institute, we found that Aaron does have a biochemical imbalance. He also has a copper and manganese imbalance. He needs to avoid sugars, chocolates, and red and yellow dyes. It's difficult because he does not want to follow the diet restrictions. He is, however, ready, willing and able to swallow a handful of supplements in order to balance out his body chemistry. I think Aaron would be making far better strides if he were to address his food sensitivities and avoid what he already knows is not healthy for him.

We have him on a natural food supplement from a company in Colorado. He is also on a regimen of assorted supplements suggested by The Pfeiffer Institute. His medications include Luvox (an anti-depressant prescribed for his OCD) and Depakote, (a mood stabilizer). He is also on Ritalin and would like to get off that entirely because it makes him feel shaky.

Our experience with the school system has taught us to document everything: calls we make or receive, appointments we make or cancel, dates we get papers in the mail, etc. We log everything according to dates and keep a file of everything we receive, plus copies of documents we have sent out. Applying for medical assistance was also important. We found out that a person has more flexibility with them if they happen to be with an HMO. We also learned that parents have a right to their children's school records. All they need to do is give the school twenty-four hours notice that they want a copy of them. We have learned so much and have become very assertive with authority figures in order to be good advocates for our son. The Whole Child Institute has helped us confirm what we were sure was true for Aaron. They are a wonderful and supportive resource to be involved with."

Aaron's experience with the Feingold Diet as a young child can be backed up by author Doug A. Kaufmann, author of *The Food Sensitivity Diet: Based On The Remarkable Scientific Breakthrough in Cytotoxic Nutrition*. Kaufmann writes, "The food sensitivity cycle starts way before a baby is born." We now know that babies can be born with inclinations toward food allergies and sensitivities. Kaufmann states, "Leading doctors, in the field of food allergy research, point to a genetic lack of specific enzymes in some individuals that makes it difficult if not impossible for them to digest certain foods. If there is not a complete lack of the enzyme, there could be a decreased amount of it, or even a malfunction in the production of the enzyme— all of which could account for a substandard digestive system and the onset of food sensitivities."

Food sensitivities often cause a child to become unable to concentrate or to have a short attention span. Many children have been diagnosed with ADD or ADHD and put on Ritalin when it may just be a food sensitivity or allergy they are dealing with. Drugs such as Ritalin, Dexedrine, and Cylert are amphetamines (speed). Drugs only mask the symptoms of why a child is dealing with hyperactivity. When a child's body is crying out for help, drugs bury the symptoms and the body's cries are silenced. It's like unscrewing the light bulb when the oil light in your car is flashing. You're not addressing the cause of the problem.

Food sensitivities and other intolerances, invisibly pave the way for future illness. In other words, whatever is causing the symptoms will continue to undermine the body. Only the discovery and temporary (until the body is balanced) elimination of an offending substance will truly help the child. Kaufmann reminds parents that if their child is taking medication and they wish to experiment with isolating his food sensitivities, it is important to work with a *nutritionally oriented* medical doctor.

Dr. Benjamin Feingold gained national attention years ago when he discovered that food additives have a physiological connection with hyperactivity in children. His view is that this condition in some people can be triggered by artificial food colorings, flavor additives, preservatives, and natural salicylates which are found in many foods. This no doubt has led to the expansion of labeling requirements. There are thousands of synthetic chemicals added to our food and none are required to be tested for the effects they could have on behavior. There are seventeen different chemicals in artificial pineapple alone!

Dr. Feingold's work has helped thousands of families dealing with their child's behavior or learning problems by teaching parents how they can easily eliminate the unwanted additives. The Feingold Association researches brand name foods and publishes books listing thousands of acceptable products, most of which can be found in supermarkets.

Parents must remember to take into account
individual differences in their children.

Families working closely with The Feingold Association report over a 90% success rate, with success being defined as a clear, noticeable improvement in symptoms, however many children will benefit further from additional therapies. That's where the Whole Child Institute can help; assisting parents as they try to fit all the puzzle pieces of a child's world together including environment and learning style.

During the teenage years it is extremely important to keep children on a healthy diet. As in Aaron's case, these are the years that young people generally begin to abuse their bodies with junk food. Experimentation with drugs, cigarettes, and alcohol can also be a problem. Food sensitivities and addiction cycles get started during these years and can change the whole course of a child's life. Kaufmann states, "Grain sensitivities can turn into alcoholism, edema, and bloating. This can set the stage for a lifetime of laziness, bad self-image, and excessive weight gain. With adequate vitamin and mineral intake their bodies start to rebuild. After a few months, they will no longer crave sugar or caffeine, doughy wheat products or salt. A donut for breakfast will look as appetizing as a mudpie and a sip of cola will meet with a wrinkled nose and lots of 'yuks.'"

In his book, *An Orthomolecular Approach To Balancing Body Chemistry*, Carl C. Pfeiffer, Ph.D., M.D. states, "In America and Britain, the incidence of violent psychopathic and antisocial behavior is rapidly rising. There is little doubt that nutritional and biochemical imbalances play a large part in behavior disorders. We know of at least nine biochemical imbalances that can result in violent behavior. It is easy to see that a diet high in sugar, additives and stimulants like coffee, and low in nutrients is associated with antisocial behavior. The very first step is to reduce sugar and junk food intake."

We believe that many of Aaron's emotional problems as a teenager, could have been helped had he strictly maintained a healthy diet. It is vitally important to consider what children put into their bodies. In cases like Aaron's, in which his susceptibility to depression led to a suicide attempt, it can be a matter of life and death.

Children with challenges can take their toll on a marriage!

Have your dreams for marriage fallen apart?

Have you been fighting and deeply hurting each other?

Do you talk, but never really communicate?

As parents, are you worried about what this is doing to your children?

Retrouvaille can help!

Retrouvaille is a program that was developed for struggling marriages…

Marriages on the rocks and even for couples who have filed for divorce or separation.

Your marriage is worth saving! Retrouvaille shows you there is hope for your marriage.

Retrouvaille Nationwide
Call: 1-800-470-2230

for a Retrouvaille weekend and follow-up group in your area of the United States.

Chapter Seven

Life with Amy was challenging even before she was born. Two months before she was due, I was flooded with anti-contraction medication. Contractions stopped after three days and two months later, she was threatening to be way overdue. She was finally born after an induced labor that only lasted five hours. She was extremely red in the face and didn't have normal coloring for almost a month.

Amy was an easy baby. As an infant she could tolerate only rice formula, but preferred breast milk. She did not like the taste of bottle nipples or pacifiers. Initially, she had been a rather sensitive child emotionally and I had to watch my tone of voice around her. She didn't become challenging, behaviorally, until she was about two and a half.

Amy was extremely weakened by all dairy products. When we removed dairy from her diet, her oppositional behavior decreased to the point where she was actually pleasant to be around. I discovered that the liver is responsible for over five hundred bodily functions and that the dairy products she was consuming were overwhelming her liver.

By age three she had taught herself to read simple words, even though she never wanted me to read to her. Amy loved to learn and always wanted to teach herself. I'll never forget watching her at age three while our babysitter tried to teach her the names of colors. She did not want to be taught, and began to shut down. She would start to ignore him, looking away and pretending he wasn't asking her questions. At one point it was obvious that I needed to intervene. I asked him to stop trying to teach her things and assured him that she would learn them on her own.

When Amy was four, her brother, Dan, came home with his first-grade reader and began to read for us. When he fumbled on a few words, she snatched it out of his hand and proceeded to read it correctly. At that time, she also understood concepts far beyond her age level, such as multiplication and only needed them defined. By age four, Amy loved to play the piano and of course she had her 'own little songs'. She played the piano at least three times a day on a regular basis so I decided to enroll her in private piano lessons. Knowing my daughter, I told the teacher to never use the word 'practice.' She agreed and Amy had a wonderful eight months of learning new material that she could play at home. As her first piano recital approached, Amy was very excited. About two weeks before the recital, her teacher made the mistake of saying, 'You know Amy, if you'd practice a little you would be even better for the recital.' That did it! That was the end of wanting to go to piano lessons until second grade; she made it through that year, recital and all. Now as an eighth grader she has no interest in playing the piano, other than to play a song from her favorite movie. Amy is a gifted musician and can quickly learn to play almost any instrument including the flute and the violin. As a parent it is frustrating raising a gifted and strong willed child.

When Amy started kindergarten, her teacher was concerned about a test she had taken. She felt Amy didn't understand the concepts being presented. It was then that I realized she was dealing with some processing challenges. I asked to have her reading level tested and she read at a fourth grade-five month level and comprehended as well as a third grader.

Even at such a young age Amy was a voracious reader, yet I began to see her love of learning slowly dying. I had heard of a behavioral optometrist who had an in-depth screening for visual integration processing—not how we see, but how we process what we see. I had Amy and her brother tested. They both had problems with reversals and other areas of visual integration processing. Amy got fifty percent wrong on the reversals test. The test was not timed and she needed to cross out all the letters and numbers that she thought were backwards.

I thought I would wait and see if Amy's visual integration processing would improve over time, because visual integration does develop as a child grows. I continued to have her visual integration processing abilities tested and she continued to get fifty percent wrong on the reversals test. By the time she turned eleven, I knew I had to do something. I had her evaluated by the same behavioral optometrist for the fourth time and this time she received a score of <u>over</u> fifty percent wrong on the reversals test. I said to my husband, 'This is not going away developmentally, we need to do something now.' We enrolled her in vision therapy and also started her on a nutritional supplement that has the ability to pass through the blood/brain barrier and pull toxins off the brain. We know of a boy who had been through vision therapy three times and his best improvement was only twenty-five percent. After two days on the supplement his eyes began to do what they should have done through all that therapy. Amy exited the vision therapy program with one hundred percent accuracy on the reversals test. Her other low scores also improved. She could use a return visit in order to strengthen a few areas. The nutritional supplement helped to balance her blood sugar and helped to detoxify her system. She was then able to consume more dairy products.

By age eleven, Amy's fixation—her ability to go from looking at her paper on her desk to the blackboard and back to her desk was that of a six-year old. Her reversal frequency was that of a six-year old as well. Her ability for visual memory was at age nine. Her motor speed was a little better than that, and her visualization and tracking were that of a twelve year old. Visualization is the ability to hold a picture in your mind and move it around. When visualization is good, usually there is good reading comprehension and good math skills. Tracking is the ability to stay on one line at a time while reading. So that explained her ability to read and comprehend, but her love of learning was dying, because she had to do a lot of flipping around in her mind to compensate for the reversals she saw.

Her poor visual integration processing skills contributed to the fact that Amy has probably had the most unique schooling background known to mankind. She asked to be homeschooled in second grade when I needed to pull her brother out of school. They also attended a homeschool co-op every other Tuesday. Dan and Amy would go to classes like music, gym, and art. I would get a break from them and be able to connect with other homeschooling parents. In third grade she choose to attend public school, but because she was signed up with a Christian homeschool co-op, the public school allowed her to be homeschooled one day a week for religious training. She decided to attend school in her fourth grade year. By October of that year, I needed to pull her out of school so she could participate in a learning therapy I had created for her brother. It is an adaptation to a program that has existed for over forty years called *Writing Road to Reading*. She worked with me for two to five minutes per day and chose to work on a twenty-subject curriculum, which she did faithfully five days a week for one month before returning to school in November.

Her social skills would drop when she was in school and rise while being homeschooled. By the end of fourth grade, her social skills had hit rock bottom and she asked to be homeschooled for fifth grade. Even though she had worked independently on a twenty-subject curriculum the one month she was homeschooled in fourth grade, during her fifth grade year she wanted nothing to do with academics. Her fourth grade teacher had encouraged me to homeschool her in fifth grade in order to improve her social skills, but also because her teacher could not find enough 'artsy' doodle time for her within the school day. So, by fifth grade, Amy was on 'sabatical' and dove headlong into arts and crafts. She worked with a family friend who taught her how to weave embroidery floss into a highly valued piece of jewelry. She took classes from a local craft store with elderly women from our area. What a wonderful key that was to raising her social skills!

Amy attended a private Christian school the last two months of fifth grade. At the beginning of sixth grade, she took the Stanford Achievement test. Four of her scores placed her at levels between ninth grade, six months (9.6) to twelfth grade,

six months (12.6). All of her other scores placed her at post-high
school levels. In fifth grade her math computation had been
fifth grade eight months (5.8) and rose to tenth grade four
months (10.4) by the end of sixth grade. As a parent I feel this
increase was due to Kumon Math and her fifth grade classroom
teacher who was willing to answer Amy's questions and help
her catch up to the class, which initially had been over a year
ahead of her.

Personology is the study of human beings through their
physical structure. Through Personology we discovered that
based on Amy's facial characteristics, she has a high need for
change. I guess that would explain her need for two bedrooms,
actually three if we consider the couch in our den, four if we
consider the couch in our family room. Once a puzzle piece is
recognized, it is easier for parents and teachers to deal with a
child.

In July of 1996, Amy and I were involved in what seemed
to be a simple car accident. Our chiropractor explained that
because our car was not dented, our bodies took as much impact
as having fallen from a two-story building. Amy's x-rays
showed that a lot had happened to her normal back and neck
alignment. She then received regular adjustments and
CranioSacral massage and showed great improvement. She
received the coveted title of Star Patient from her chiropractor.
When asked to write about her experience, in the star patient
log, Amy wrote, 'I was moody, hyper, and oppositional.
Through Contact Reflex Analysis sm (CRAsm) my chiropractor
discovered that my thyroid was weak and nutritionally deficient.
She put me on, a nutritional supplement to support my thyroid
and I was much easier to get along with, which my family
appreciated.' In seventh grade she wrote, 'I am currently dealing
with a lung allergy which has prevented me from running in
gym class due to shortness of breath. I was concerned about
possibly developing asthma. My chiropractor tested me again
through CRA and has recommended nutritional supplements
which are helping to strengthen my lungs.'

Amy had a rough time getting out of bed in the mornings during her seventh grade year. Having gym class first hour didn't help the situation. The nutritional therapies she had that year allowed her to be a 'normal teenager', junk food and all. Amy's dairy allergy is now only a sensitivity and contributes to some oppositional/defiant behavior if she consumes too much yellow cheese or ice cream.

Last year before seventh grade I enrolled her in another public school district, other than our own, until she graduates. Her junior high teachers have been wonderful and her school nurse should get a medal for her wonderful, patient support, through Amy's trying seventh grade year.

These days, beginning of eighth grade, Amy boasts of having 150 friends, which is a great improvement from her grade school days. If she misses school, our home is flooded with phone calls from her friends asking, 'Amy, where were you today?' and comments like, 'We missed you!'

Life with Amy is no longer as challenging as it used to be. She now has enough energy to be on her school dance line team and this past winter was involved once a week with the downhill ski club. Her father and I are learning how to deal with 'normal' teenage behavior".

Putting the Puzzle Pieces Together—by Linda Vettrus

I went to the Twin Cities Autism Society Conference one year where a speaker from Boston was sharing research she had performed along with research from all over the world. She talked about a study that was done on infant monkeys. Researchers had removed the amygdala and hippocampus from the brains of infant monkeys. These parts of the brain lie just behind the ears. She said at first the monkeys who had these parts removed seemed fine, but then it was noticed that the monkeys were not developing like their peers. Eventually, they displayed full-blown signs of autism such as, no eye contact or social interaction as if they were in a world of their own. When they removed only one of the two sections of the brain instead of both, they displayed symptoms of ADD and when they removed the opposite section, the monkeys developed symptoms of ADHD. Through the Whole Child Institute I have seen so many kids pull out of ADD and ADHD symptoms that it really makes me wonder how many toxins must be lying on the brains of children today, particularly in the area of the hippocampus and amygdala. I was told at the conference that in the future, as a society, we would no longer be hearing as much about ADD and ADHD as we will autism since it is on the rise by twenty-five percent.

My daughter Amy and my son Dan are classic examples of children who have dealt with toxins in their brains. After watching the movie Lorenzo's Oil and what I learned about the infant monkey studies, I am more convinced than ever that children today are dealing with toxins in their brains as well as in their bodies. Through the Whole Child Institute and by observing the work of other professionals, I have witnessed many children pulling out from under labels such as ADD/ADHD, Autism, ODD, etc. As in Lorenzo's Oil, I have witnessed the pursuit of parent's educating professionals along the way to discovering how to help their child. Like Mr. and Mrs. Lorenzo, I also advocate the networking of parents and professionals. I believe that parents should be considered the most knowledgeable professional when it comes to their child.

Together we can make a difference!

Chapter Eight

Although this book is not about children with cancer, we felt this story was valuable for teaching ways to prevent chronic illness and create healthy families. Diane Hicks shares her painful story in order to help parents and caregivers understand the importance of diet and environmental pollutants.

"My second son Matthew was born in February, 1975 weighing a slight six pounds, seven ounces. Although his older brother Scott, had weighed over eight pounds, I wasn't too alarmed by Matthew's lower birth weight. What did concern me was that he didn't gain weight after he was born. By the age of one month, he still weighed only six pounds. At six months of age, just barely weighing ten pounds, he was still wearing newborn clothing and as a teenager he grew to five foot two and weighed only about 100 pounds.

There were evidences of digestive problems early on in Matthew's life. Milk with more than 2% milk fat would give him a rash or he would get hives after eating something he was unaccustomed to. Gradually, we learned the things that Matthew could and could not eat. He never ate much meat, but preferred fruits and vegetables, and was constantly complimenting people on their wonderful vegetables if we went somewhere for dinner.

We lived out in the country of Montana where I often took my boys camping and hiking. They became very comfortable with the wilderness. I know now though, that rural Montana is not so pristine as one might imagine. There were planes flying overhead spraying the fields, and sometimes the cloud of chemicals would drift into our yard. We liked to watch the planes so we would go out and watch them totally unaware of what we were exposing ourselves to. The children would swim in the ditches, creeks and reservoirs full of irrigation water. It wasn't until much later that I became concerned about pesticide and herbicide residues contaminating the water my children were swimming in. Our drinking water came from a well which more than likely contained chemicals that had trickled down through the soil along with the water. I'm sure we had pretty 'hefty' doses of toxic chemicals in our well water.

One day when Matthew was ten, he started throwing up. After three days I took him to a pediatrician because I was concerned about him getting dehydrated. I figured he probably had a virus, yet I thought it was odd that his temperature had remained normal. After he threw up, he could eat as much food as a full-grown man and was happy to. He didn't seemed to feel sick after he threw up. The doctor couldn't really find anything initially, but called me on a daily basis to check on Matthew. After three weeks, Matthew was still vomiting so much that he couldn't go to school. I called the doctor and said, 'Something is really wrong with Matthew.' His doctor scheduled him for some tests and the following day it was determined that he had a brain tumor. It was a medulloblastoma, and it was pushing on the nerves that controlled his stomach.

Surgery was scheduled and on Monday, October 14, 1985, Matthew awoke from surgery a violently ill ten year old boy. He couldn't see. He was having hallucinations brought about by his pain medication. Amazingly enough, he remembered the surgery! He said he had heard what had gone on during his operation and described it all in detail to me over the days to come. On Wednesday, the surgeon talked to me and told me he had recommended Matthew for the Make-A-Wish program. I said, 'Let me clarify this.' 'Are you trying to tell me my son is going to die?' He said there was a 60% chance that Matthew would be dead within five years, but he certainly would not reach adulthood. Of course this news was devastating to me, but for Matthew's sake I felt I needed to stay in control. I decided I couldn't break down in front of Matthew because he was relying on me. Fortunately, because of his surgical bandages, he couldn't see, so I sat there with tears running down my face next to his hospital bed.

Matthew had about three to four weeks of whole head and spinal radiation. He was given experimentally high doses of radiation, which hit every major organ, causing considerable damage. It was a horrible process. Matthew's weight went down to about 50 lbs., and he vomited constantly. The surgery had removed about 80% of the tumor. After the radiation treatments there was nothing but scar tissue left.

We discovered The Big Sky Kids, a wonderful cancer support group, where Matthew could always go and totally be himself. He remained a member of the Big Sky Kids the rest of his life. After he was too old to be an actual 'kid' he was a counselor to other kids that joined. Matthew made friends from all over the world through that organization.

Matthew went back to school for sixth grade and enjoyed a fairly normal childhood. At the age of seventeen, however, he started having trouble with the back of his hip and within a few months there was a visible lump. He wouldn't allow doctors to touch it because it was so painful, but an x-ray showed that it was a second primary osteogenic sarcoma. We began treatment immediately, including chemotherapy and surgery. The doctors had to remove all of the affected bone. Physically and mentally Matthew had a difficult time dealing with his surgery, but eventually, he began to walk again and came home from the hospital.

Matthew was not gaining weight and we felt we had to get him to eat something, anything. He had started a burger and pop diet, working at a fast food restaurant; he loved that stuff. He always had a soda in his hand. He ate chips and salty things. He liked nuts and other fast food. We thought he ate well and encouraged him to eat by serving the foods he liked—basically junk food.

In April of 1994 he finished his cancer treatment. He did not return to the doctor for a check up until a year later when it was discovered that he had tumors in his lungs that couldn't be removed surgically. They told us that he probably had less than a year to live. Previously, Matthew had called a friend who has, so far, survived two years longer than expected after receiving diet and nutritional therapy. He was healthy and doing a tour of the US visiting Big Sky Kids groups. At that time, he encouraged Matthew to go to a clinic and begin nutritional therapy. Matthew said if nothing else worked, he would do it. He wasn't willing to give up his diet of burgers, chicken wings and sodas, and begin taking supplements. Eventually he did see a nutritionist and started some supplements and dietary changes, but at that stage of his disease, there were times when he couldn't even swallow water because the tumors would push on his esophagus.

Together Matthew and I read books on treating cancer nutritionally. We learned about food allergies. I admitted him to the Cancer Treatment Center of America. They began to feed him the way he should have been fed all along. They use a saline based solution in their nutrient formulas. They don't use a glucose based nutrient formula like almost every other hospital because glucose feeds cancer and increases the numbers of metastases dramatically. When Matthew learned this, he undoubtedly pictured in his mind all the sodas and junk food he had eaten and he looked at me and said, 'Oh Mom, I did it to myself.' We just didn't know any better.

One day, after weeks of chemotherapy and transfusions, Matthew's liver shut down. In June of 1996, he became ventilator dependent. He wasn't willing to live that way, so I told him it could be turned off. He nodded, it was turned off and he died.

Knowing that Matthew had an inability to metabolize food properly from the time he was born, I often wonder—had we known how to eat properly, would we have made a better effort to get proper nutrition into him. We may have been able to postpone his getting cancer. I am not sure we could have entirely prevented it though, because cancer is a disease brought about by not only an impaired immune system due to lack of good nutrition, but also by environmental and emotional stressors as well.

After Matthew's death, I was thankful upon discovering the Whole Child Institute when I needed help for my son Jonathan, born eleven years after Matthew, in April of 1986. He was one of my fattest little babies, and very happy. Everyone enjoyed him! He was a problem free baby until about the age of eighteen months, when he began having trouble sleeping at night. At first I wasn't too concerned, but then it developed into a habit. Even though he didn't sleep well at night he seemed happy and was well behaved during the day, so there didn't seem to be any reason to do something about it.

Jonathan got his first ear infection when he was three months old. Thereafter he would have four to six ear infections a year. By the time he was about nine, his doctors were talking about surgery. He had repeated rounds of antibiotics that became more expensive because he developed tolerances to them. Eventually it cost me $150 per prescription, which wasn't covered by my insurance policy.

His first three years of school were frustrating. He didn't like school from the beginning. When he was in second grade I was not told until parent teacher conferences that he had been misbehaving in class. He had been jumping on the teacher's desk, and hitting children on the playground, yet I was assured at the conference that he was not doing these things anymore. He had never acted like that at home, so I was concerned. I began volunteering at the school two mornings a week, so I could see what was going on. Jonathan would fall off his chair, peel the paint off his pencil, and after two hours, he would produce only one word on his paper. He wasn't being naughty, he just wasn't doing what he was asked to do. His class had about eight other children who displayed attention deficits and I felt the teacher could not teach effectively in this atmosphere. I had a lot of experience with children, my own, my husband's from his previous marriage, my daycare kids and the children I worked with through summer Vacation Bible schools , yet I had never seen one like Jonathan.

The school wanted to test him for ADHD. I refused because I wanted to be sure that it was not the result of just a lot of stress and not really ADHD. His older brother after all was dealing with cancer at the time and because of it, our family life suffered horribly. His school was not willing to give me the time I needed, so I put him into a Montessori School where Jonathan progressed a little bit. I had him tested sometime later and although he *did not* receive an ADHD diagnosis, it was recommended that he receive Special Education services and work with an Occupational Therapist at his school. I was satisfied with the findings.

After Matthew died, Jonathan had a traumatic experience when visiting his biological father. I took him to a psychologist and I suggested that we address the possibility of ADHD at the same time. I told her I hadn't had problems with him being hyperactive, but they did have problems with him at school not being able to sit still. After testing him he was found to be dealing with ADHD.

I went to a Community Education Class about ADHD presented by Allen Becker. It was there that I was introduced to the possibility of natural ways for treating ADHD. I also received a brochure about the Whole Child Institute. I was interested in hearing about how they worked with these kids. Along with Ritalin, Jonathan was on Clonidine patches, which are suppose to help with hyperactivity because Clonidine is a sedative, but it doesn't do anything for the attention deficit problem. I started him on a natural food supplement soon after the class. When his Clonidine patch ran out, the hyperactivity and nervous ticks he had been experiencing before wearing the patch, were gone. He will have to remain on Ritalin for a short time while I am exploring diet, allergies, and natural supplements to replace any medical intervention he might need to have.

Jonathan wasn't born with hyperactivity and skin sensitivities and all the other problems that he has had. Everything seemed to have developed after he was a year old, so I feel optimistic that we can reverse his downward spiral with the help of a healthy diet and possibly other alternative therapies. I eliminated milk from his diet in June of 1996. This was a difficult step for me, the granddaughter of a dairy farmer, but now he says it doesn't even taste good. Jonathan hasn't had a single ear infection since then. He is also getting counseling and as I pull myself together again I'll be able to help Jonathan organize himself. As he gets closer to being eleven years old his hormones are beginning to kick in. I'm seeing more and more preteen behavioral problems and I know that it will be a challenge to keep him to a healthy lifestyle."

Diane's story is a long and terrible journey into the realization that our diet has a direct impact on our health. One can only wonder who Matthew would have been now if he had turned to nutritional therapy earlier, or if his family had known how important a proper diet is to good health.

Diane's experience with her son Matthew has helped her to make healthier choices for her son Jonathan, with his completely different array of challenges, as well as for her other children.

Chapter Nine

As Dr. Sehnert stated in the foreword of our book, being mothers of special needs children, we earned "Ph.D.s" in the "College of Hard Knocks". While working with our own families as well as others, we discovered that toxicity has been the number one factor causing many children to become challenging.

What in our world today isn't toxic? Toxicity is everywhere, in the air we breathe, in the water we drink, in the foods we eat, and in the medications we take. Our cleaning products as well as our personal care products can also be highly toxic. We even need to be concerned about the affects electromagnetic fields and fluorescent lighting may have on our health.

It is a known fact that infants today encounter 80,000 germs at birth. In their book, *Raising Children Toxic Free* Herbert L. Needleman, M.D. and Phillip J. Landrigan, M.D. state, "The children of today face hazards that were neither known nor imagined just two decades ago. Since 1950, at least 70,000 new chemical compounds have been invented and disbursed into our environment through new consumer commodities, industrial products and foods. Only a fraction of these have been tested for human toxicity. We are by default conducting a massive clinical toxicological trial; our children and their children are the experimental animals." The Whole Child Institute is concerned about the effects that these environmental and societal factors have on the health and well being of children.

Doris Rapp, M.D. has come to our nation's rescue with her book, *Is This Your Child's World?* She explains in detail environmental toxicity and how to create a less toxic home environment. This book is a "must-read" for anyone concerned about children's health today.

Children are more vulnerable to the toxins in our world than adults. Their little bodies are like sponges and absorb a greater amount of many substances through their intestinal tract and lungs. For example, a child would absorb about half of the lead they swallow, while an adult would absorb only about one-tenth. Children transfer more foreign substances into their bodies because they indulge in more hand-to-mouth activity than adults. Doctors, Needleman and Landrigan, state that, "Children take in more air, food and water per pound of body weight than adults." Since a child's immune system is less developed than an adult's they are more vulnerable to the countless toxins in our world. The developing cells in a child are usually more susceptible. than mature cells, particularly in the central nervous system. The brain develops at an extraordinary rate during fetal life and continues until approximately age three. Exposure to small doses of neurotoxins can affect developing brain connections prenatally, making it very important for anyone considering having children to make every effort to control the amount of toxins in their world.

According to the Minneapolis Star Tribune, Sunday April 6th, 1997, an article entitled *Living With Illness*, written by H.J. Cummins, states "One in four American youngsters has at least one *chronic illness*." At the Whole Child Institute we ask, *"Why?"* *"What is at the cause and core of this staggering statistical fact?"* In this chapter we intend to educate our readers concerning the variety of dangers children may face in their homes and schools everyday, beginning with the air they breathe.

Air—We all know that outdoor air pollution is a serious problem, but did you know that the Environmental Protection Agency as well as the United States House of Representatives calls *indoor air pollution* the number one environmental health problem in America today? American's spend 90% of their time indoors breathing potential contaminants.

The average American home is built for efficient climate control, keeping air from moving through the house. Porous materials such as styrene, fiberglass, and wood can accumulate disease causing pollutants. Duct-work can be full of mold, mildew, dust, and bacteria due to inadequate ventilation. When you look through a ray of sunshine, 80% of what you see floating in the air is dead skin from people who have been in the room. Dust and dirt are trapped in the pads of carpets and bedding. Dust mites live close to their food source, which is dead skin and their excrement is highly prone to cause allergic reactions. When we put two and two together, we realize that our own beds can become a "cafeteria" and breeding ground for these tiny creatures! Doctors say that, "dust is the last great medium of human infection" because airborne germs have no way of travelling except by attaching themselves to dust particles.

Nature has a very unique way of cleansing the air with ozone, a powerful oxidizing agent which reduces contaminants to harmless natural substances. This is hard to duplicate by increasing ventilation or using home air filters, which actually filter only about 10% of the air in a home.

Simple solutions to indoor air pollution include increasing the number of houseplants in one's home, using a high quality home air filtering system or using essential oils in a diffuser. Essential oils contain anti-fungal and anti-bacterial properties and can be diffused into the air by a small machine called a diffuser. For individuals who are sensitive to indoor air pollution it is important to increase the amount of time spent outdoors.

Petroleum—is a major air pollutant that our children are exposed to everyday. The exhaust from cars and buses lined up and left running in front of schools can cause illness and behavior problems in children. Some schools line up buses at the end of the day and leave them running for fifteen to twenty minutes until they are boarded by children and ready to leave. We have seen children in wheelchairs sitting outside, close to the running buses, while the wind blew the bus fumes right into their faces! Children who are driven to daycare everyday are exposed to a lot of petroleum fumes, especially if parents leave their vehicles running while dropping them off or while going in to get them. People leave their cars running when they are stopped at hotels loading or unloading their suitcases and young children have been seen standing in a cloud of fumes. Sadly, parents don't realize these fumes can be harming their children and that they need to protect them from these situations. These practices are even more detrimental in the winter when cold air is thinner, allowing toxins to move through it faster. Thus, people are exposed to more concentrated levels of pollution in cold weather.

Anna Kruger, in her book *ecoHome,* states that Benzene is a toxic chemical, which in high doses is carcinogenic. It is found primarily in unleaded gasoline and is a proven cause of leukemia and lymphoma. Benzene can be absorbed into the body through the skin and is present in many everyday products. Unfortunately, Benzene *is not* listed on product labels. Avoid exposing children to this toxin whenever possible by using all-natural, safe, personal hygiene products.

Radon—is a radioactive gas that is colorless and odorless. According to Dr. Herbert Needleman, "Radon gas seeps into houses from the rock and soil beneath and from ground water supplies that pass through radon-rich rock and are piped into homes. It is nine times heavier than air, so it tends to collect in the basement, or the lowest part of the house if there is no basement. Radon gas has been linked to diseases such as leukemia, skin and kidney cancers as well as some childhood cancers. Radon may have a synergistic effect with cigarette smoke, which can double the risk of lung cancer. Those who smoke, or who live with smokers are at a higher risk if radon is present in their homes."

If you are concerned that radon gas is a problem in your home, there are some steps you can take to reduce the risk. The book, *eco-HOME,* suggests making sure that your basement is thoroughly ventilated, and any cracks in the floor or walls are sealed. Open a window while showering, and install vents in the walls or ceiling to ensure a good supply of fresh air in the bathroom.

Lead—is known to interfere with a child's ability to learn and can potentially cause brain damage in children, while in adults, it may only cause nerve damage. Unfortunately, most of us have lead in our bodies because we have been exposed to it through air, food, or water.

We are exposed to lead in paint chips, and paint dust released into the air during remodeling, as well as through lead solder used in water pipes or food cans. Even leaded glassware and dishes can have a detrimental effect on our health. It is important to check any paint applied to buildings prior to 1980 for lead content.

Early symptoms of lead poisoning can include: Abdominal pain, anemia, nausea, vomiting, loss of appetite, constipation, headaches, dizziness, poor coordination, memory loss, clumsiness, muscle pains, muscle weakness, cramps, irritability, depression, problems in seeing or hearing, numbness and tingling, a metallic taste in the mouth, excessive thirst, insomnia, lethargy, and seizures. Dr. Doris Rapp states, "Lead can also cause a permanent decrease in IQ and attention span, hyperactivity and difficulties in walking or writing." Lead poisoning can easily be misdiagnosed because chemical sensitivity and ADHD can cause similar symptoms. It does not require very much exposure to lead to cause illness, speech impairment, and learning difficulties in some people.

In *Raising Children Toxic Free,* Doctors. Needleman and Landrigan state, "There is pervasive evidence that some hyperactive behavior is an expression of disordered brain function." It has already been established that neurotoxins can and do play a role in attention and behavioral disorders. Lead provides one example. In American and British studies it has been shown that lead affects many of the sensitive areas in the brain that regulate behavior. It has also been found that some of these exposures may occur before birth, because lead has the ability to cross the placental barrier. Infants inside the womb are exposed to lead if their mother's levels become increased.

To check for lead poisoning, you can request a blood test

called an FEP, or Free Erythrocyte Protoporphyrine. This will help determine if you need to have a more specific test done to verify that lead is actually the problem. Hair analysis and abdominal x-rays are also helpful in detecting lead.

Water—In her book, *Is This Your Child's World?,* Doris Rapp, M.D. states, "The most common contaminants in water would be germs or sewage, chemicals both industrial and agricultural and possibly radiation and lead. Industrial chemicals are the source for about 45% of the major pollution in water. If these chemicals enter the body and cannot be eliminated, they tend to be stored in body fat. Depending on how long one is exposed to these toxins and considering individual tendencies, these substances can cause serious illnesses in some people."

Although chlorine is added to water to reduce the number of germs, it can actually be the cause of some illnesses. Fluorides, which are chemically similar to chlorides or bromides, are found in many urban water supplies. It is claimed to decrease dental cavities, but a number of articles and books have been published that dispel this claim and expose the potentially adverse effects of fluoride. The water that comes into our homes through public access systems is generally impure and contaminated from run-off of pesticides in our soil and garbage that collects in our lakes and rivers. Lawn and aerial herbicide sprays can seep into ground water, cisterns, wells, and reservoirs. Although diluted, these contaminants can eventually come right out of the kitchen faucet!

Radon contaminates not only the air in some homes, but it can greatly affect the water supply. Radon from ground water supplies finds its way into tap water and can concentrate in the bathroom where the vapor may be released from the shower in a fine spray. It then breaks down, emitting tiny particles that are easily absorbed by the lung tissue causing serious damage, or even exacerbating an existing asthma condition. A Canadian study revealed that radon levels increased rapidly during a short warm shower, and the gas was not dispersed until ninety minutes later! In-line water filters that reduce levels of radon in water systems are now available.

As parents and consumers we should tolerate absolutely no amount of lead in any school or home water supply. Water that flows through lead soldered pipes or fountains can be contaminated with lead. If water sits inside a pipe for a long time, a greater amount of lead will leech into it. Many people are misled to think that merely running the water before drinking it will make it safe to drink. There is also a potential for copper and zinc to be present in pipes and it is important to test for proper levels of metals by blood or hair analysis especially in sick children.

There is treatment for lead poisoning with a drug called EDTA (Ethylene Diamine Tetracetate) which combines with lead in the body so that the kidneys can excrete it. Also, some antioxidants have been known to decrease lead levels, however, this kind of treatment should be pursued with the supervision of a natural healthcare professional.

Testing—You can check your own water by requesting current reports from your water and health departments. Ask if chlorine and/or flouride is added to the water and what kinds of pipes are used to transport the water in your area. You might want to ask for a map of the toxic dump sites in your area. Check to see if they are near the municipal water supply source. We would like to trust the EPA to protect us from hazards like this, but they only monitor eight inorganic and ten organic chemicals in our water supplies. That leaves checking for at least 30,000 other unregulated and potentially hazardous pollutants. Some water supplies can also have parasites like Giardia or the organisms that cause Legionnairs' Disease. It is possible to get an independent analysis of your water if you believe it is warranted. For chemical testing, you can contact a laboratory called Accu-Chem, and for germ or parasite testing contact a University Bacteriology or Parasitology Department or your Health Department.

Unfortunately, your water might have to be tested more than once, because the samples can vary from day to day depending upon the level of detectable contaminants. Some companies will purposely dump their waste into the air or our water supplies on the weekends in order to decrease their chances of getting caught polluting over their limits.

Purifying Water—Our bodies are mostly made up of water, so to maintain good health, we need to drink a lot of pure water each day. The constant use of impure water can affect the health of children to the point where they cannot learn. As parents, we must find the purest water possible for our children. Water can be purified in many different ways. Distilled water for instance can create health difficulties because valuable minerals can be lost. Distilled water pulls minerals out of the body *indiscriminately,* so the bad minerals are pulled out as well as the good. Remember to take mineral supplements when drinking distilled water. Anyone dealing with a seizure disorder should be extremely careful to work with a doctor and slowly introduce mineral supplements. Mineral baths seem to be a good way to begin the process. People may start drinking distilled water in order to detoxify, but if they stay on it too long, they can get sicker without mineral supplementation. Magnesium and calcium are especially important minerals that can be lost in the distillation process.

Reverse-osmosis is another way to purify water. Yet like distilled water, water purified by this process may intensify a mineral deficiency in some people. Water purified by reverse-osmosis is known to be very pure. Distilled water and water purified by reverse-osmosis are usually safe to drink if consumers understand the importance of mineral supplementation. Our food these days is also mineral deficiant, so supplementation is crucial.

You can find out more about problems caused by water in Volume I of *Chemical Sensitivy* by William Rea, M.D. and more about lead contamination and hazards through The National Lead Information Center.

Food—Another form of pollution, are food additives. Many parents testify that their children exhibit improved health and behavior on a diet free from them. It has, however, been difficult to adequately prove because in many scientific studies on children, compliance with the diet is a very big problem. It is difficult for the parents and children involved in the study to stick to a special diet and a lot of times, they just drop out and do not complete it.

Test tube studies however, show food colorings to damage nerve tissue, and it has been discovered that many food reactions in children are due to a whole range of naturally existing chemicals along with food additives.

Robert Buist, M.D. wrote, *Food Chemical Sensitivity* and he States, "While food colors and food additives have been implicated for a long time as a major cause of hyperactivity, other factors in the environment may also be responsible for hyperactive behavior." He explains that it may not be just sensitivity to a food or an environmental pollutant that causes behavioral problems, but the combination of the two working together. This is why, at the Whole Child Institute, we feel it is important to look at all of the"pieces" of a child's life in order to get the whole picture of what the child is really dealing with.

Dr. Buist also notes that Benjamin Urshoff from the Institute of Nutritional Studies in Culver City, CA has shown that food additives may be more toxic when ingested together rather than if they are taken separately. His studies suggest a definite toxic interaction between different substances such as food dyes, sweeteners, and surface wetting agents.

Our society today consumes nutritionally deficient foods and beverages. Take a few moments to think about what is going into your child's body. It is not uncommon for schools to allow students to drink soda pop. On almost any given morning teens as well as staff can be seen 'sluggin one down' for breakfast. Since the 1940's American diets have taken a dive into poor nutrition. Scientists have noted that our diets were more deficient after we began using more food additives, colorings, and pesticides. In more recent years, an interesting study was done with cats. Dr. Frances M. Pottenger was interested in how diet affected certain laboratory animals. He noticed that the diets of wild cats included the consumption of small animals soon after the cats had killed them. In his study, he fed two groups of cats differing diets. One group received raw milk and raw meat. The other group, received cooked meat and milk that had been pasteurized. The group with the raw diet flourished, while the second group eating cooked foods began having health problems. They had miscarriages, their mothering behavior began to deteriorate, and their coats became rough and dull. They eventually reproduced; although they died sooner than they normally would have. Their offspring, the second generation, showed signs of poor health. They were so high strung and vicious they had to be handled with protective gear. Their kittens were born with skeletal malformations. The third generation was sickly as well as ugly. Their hair was falling out and they were scraggly looking. This third generation of cats was unable to reproduce, so *the fourth generation never happened.* Dr. Pottenger's research shows the effects a diet of processed foods had on his laboratory animals. It's scary to imagine what implications our own nutritional habits may have on our children and their futures. Since we don't know the long-term effects that a diet of completely processed foods will have on us, we are all truly part of a vast experiment in highly industrialized living. Note: We are not suggesting that humans should eat raw or partially cooked meat.

Doris Rapp, M.D. is discouraged by the lack of acceptance in the medical community concerning the possibility that food, water, and environmental sensitivities could be causing behavioral, learning and/or health problems in our children. Since there are medical textbooks on the subject of food and water sensitivities dating back to the early 1900's, it doesn't make any sense at all that in general, the medical community is resistant to believing there is a connection. Even more evidence is documented in an astounding number of contemporary articles, books, and videotapes that confirm the roles food and water play in causing many behavioral and learning problems. Dr. Rapp states, "About 8 million of the 53 million Americans under the age of 18 now suffer from some kind of emotional, behavioral, or mental disorder." The American Academy of Pediatrics found a 2.5 fold increase in the prevalence of methylphyenidate (Ritalin) treatment for children between 1990 and 1995.

There is no curriculum in teachers' colleges or medical universities that we are aware of to educate professionals concerning the effects of food and water sensitivities in their students and patients. Fortunately, there is an ever-increasing number of professionals including teachers, psychologists, and doctors who are *educating themselves* about the connections between nutrition and behavior.

Aspartame—The world's most controversial sweetener, also known as NutraSweet/Equal™, is arguably the most toxic substance in our food supply today. Mary Nash Stoddard, author of Deadly Deception—Story of Aspartame, understands this statement first hand. Mary founded the worldwide anti-aspartame consumer movement following the devastating reaction to the sweetener suffered by her youngest child in 1985. Beginning with debilitating migraine headaches, progressing into severe heart problems, and culminating in a grand mal seizure on a school field trip; the symptoms disappeard following cessation of ingestion of a kool aid type sugar free drink her daughter liked. Her child's reaction sent Stoddard on a thirteen year campaign to warn parents of the dangers associated with use of the sweetener in sugar-free products.

Some of the medical conditions Aspartame may exacerbate or mimic include: Epilepsy, Attention Deficit Disorder, Chronic Fatigue, Fibromyalgia, Depression, Systemic Lupus, Alzheimer's (affecting long and short term memory), Multiple Sclerosis, Lyme Disease, Heart Ailments, and bizarre psychological and behavioral disorders. Aspartame disease is a real epidemic in our world and must be stopped.

Whole Child Institute

Mary Nash Stoddard has a professional background in broadcast and print media. She is a popular keynote speaker and author. Ms. Stoddard's Deadly Deception—Story of Aspartame is available to order by calling: 1-800-969-6050

Electromagnetic Fields—As if all these environmental and nutritional problems aren't enough for parents and health professionals to deal with everyday, there remains two more topics of concern, electromagnetic fields or EMF's and fluorescent lighting. EMF's are a kind of atmospheric pollution that we have to consider inside and outside our homes. An electromagnetic field is simply an area of energy around an electrical power source, or an electrical appliance. Most of us are familiar with the fact that very strong EMF's exist near overhead power lines, but we must also be aware that the electric cables coming into our homes as well as the many electrical appliances we use such as T.V.'s and personal computers can create EMF's. Cell phones and pagers play a dramatic role in our health today seeing that most people wear them and/or touch them throughout their day.

According to *eco-HOME's* author Anna Kruger, the symptoms from EMF exposure are called "electro-stress." EMF's can disrupt the body's natural electrical impulses, and exposure to EMF's has been proven to damage the immune system and can interfere with behavior patterns and a child's general development.

There are some precautions everyone can take inside their homes to curtail the emission of these energy fields. Basically, the closer you are to an electrical appliance, the stronger the field. Parents should realize that the highest exposure to electromagnetic radiation, in most homes, comes from turning electrical switches on and off. Consider not allowing sensitive children to turn on or off appliances like the T.V. or the computer. If you or your children use a personal computer, make sure others stay as far from the sides and back of the monitor as possible, since this is where most of the energy emission comes from. Installing a special computer screen may help to limit EMF's.

Installing a demand switch in bedrooms will cut the electrical current when it is not needed. Avoiding waterbeds (heaters) and not using electric blankets may prove to be helpful measures.

Elsewhere in the house, EMF's may exist around the area where a cord is plugged into the wall. An easy solution to this is to keep unused appliances unplugged in order to avoid electromagnetic radiation leakage.

Fluorescent Lighting—Our last environmental problem for consideration is fluorescent lighting. The best possible lighting for schools or anywhere, is natural lighting. Many children sit under fluorescent lights for at least six hours during their school day. Many after school childcare centers and obviously latchkey programs within the schools have children under fluorescent lighting. Dr. Doris Rapp states in her book *Is This Your Child's World?*, "Ordinary fluorescent lights can emit x-rays, radiation, and radio waves—emissions that can decrease productivity and cause fatigue, confusion, eyestrain, irritability, depression, and hyperactivity in some sensitive children." Dr. Rapp reccomends ultra-violet lighting when sunlight is not available. She notes that, "Germany banned fluorescent lights in both schools and hospitals years ago;..." For further reading on lighting she suggests John Otts books and Irene Wilkenfeld's discussion on the many aspects of light in *The Healthy School Handbook.*

By means of the Whole Child Institute many parents of challenging children have discovered that toxicity is one of the root causes for behavioral and learning problems. Parents often don't realize their options and are not educated concerning cause and core reasons for why their child or children are difficult. During a whole child assessment many pieces of a child's puzzle are put together. Parents begin to learn what their child is really dealing with. The stories in this book document what can happen when families look beyond a child's symptoms to their cause and core and are given resources, which empower them to help their child.

Chapter Ten

At the Whole Child Institute, nutrition is only one piece of the puzzle we consider when helping a child with challenges and their family. For this reason, we will briefly discuss some points on nutrition and explain how nutrition is more than food.

We believe that nutrition is needed on more than just a physical plane. Nourishing our bodies and brains goes far beyond food, liquids, and vitamin or mineral supplements. We will address here the importance of getting enough oxygen, drinking pure water, eating proper food and getting enough exercise. Nutrition for our minds and souls will be discussed later in this chapter. But first, we will discuss some physical aspects of nutrition.

Breathing—We all know that oxygen is absolutely essential for life. Without oxygen, nutrients cannot be fully assimilated by the body, leaving us nutritionally deficient. Therefore, breathing is a fundamental part of our existence. We all know how refreshing a few deep breaths can be. Teaching children to take a few minutes during their day to do some deep breathing, can bring about better attention and a calmer more balanced body. Slow, deep, gentle breathing can relieve stress, lower blood pressure, calm fears, and clear the mind. Taking a few minutes to jump on a mini trampoline is good for the limbic system and gets oxygen circulating throughout the body. Although we obviously never overlook this elementary factor in our nutrition, we often fail to use this source of nutrition to its fullest.

Water—Next in importance for general health is pure water. We discussed the need for pure water in the chapter entitled

"Our Toxic World." If a person is drinking an ample amount of water daily, there will not be as much room to consume other less beneficial beverages such as coffee, sodas, and concentrated fruit juices. Muscle testing has revealed that many children with behavioral or learning challenges need anywhere from 9 to 12 cups of pure water per day. Children with really suppressed systems seem to need up to 14 cups per day. Always contact your child's medical practitioner to ensure you have chosen the correct amount of water for your child. Our bodies are electrical and water contains electrolytes. Water is like a brain-food that refuels the batteries of the brain. By drinking water throughout the day children can learn and think more clearly.

In *Your Body's Many Cries For Water*, Dr. F. Batmanghellidj stresses how much the brain and body require water. Not only do the kidneys need enough liquid to excrete bodily wastes, but this doctor also claims that asthma, arthritis, stress, and low-back pain can be helped by drinking plenty of pure water. He recommends two quarts per day for adults.

Medication vs. Herbs, Vitamins, Minerals, and Bioflavanoids—It has been noted by an authority on herbs that it takes approximately one month of herbal treatment to correct a year's worth of an ailment. Translated into practical terms the earlier in life one incorporates holistic therapy the faster change can take place and the earlier wellness can be accomplished. It is important to note that herbs are only one step down in being safer than medication. The hierarchy of safety is as follows...

More potential side effects:	Medication
	Herbs
	Vitamins
	Minerals
Less potential side effects:	Bioflavanoids

Daily Diet—The daily diet is an important and timely topic in our American culture. On one end there are people who are literally "digging their graves with their teeth," and never stop to consider whether something they eat is nutritious. At the other end are those who are so fanatical about what they eat; they are unable to relax and enjoy their food. We would suggest a balanced attitude toward food and nutrition and this chapter serves to help our readers find that balance.

We tend to thrive on foods that come directly from our basic energy sources—earth, air, sun, and water. The challenge we face today is that our air and water are so polluted and the earth so depleted of minerals that the nutrition we do get is greatly undermined. This is one argument for the use of food supplements; herbs, vitamins, and minerals taken in pill form to supplement our daily food intake. Dr. Michael Colgan reports that, "Until the 1940's, farmers returned essential nutrients to the soil." Today only three nutrients are returned to the soil. Dr. Colgan also states that, "Humans need more than nitrogen, phosphorus, and potassium. They need selenium, chromium, calcium, magnesium, iron, copper, iodine, molybdenum, zinc, cobalt, boron and vanadium." Today it would take approximately seventy-five cups of spinach to equal the nutrition of one cup back in 1948. Who could eat seventy-five cups of spinach? The need to supplement the daily diet is greater than ever.

The closer to its natural state, the more nutritious food is likely to be. For this reason, we suggest avoiding processed foods as much as possible. If the ingredient list is more than four lines long, or is too difficult to pronounce, one might consider putting that product back on the store shelf. Check to see if more than one sweetener is listed or if the product contains food dyes or preservatives like BHT, MSG, or BHA. These are red flag items that signal a nutritionally poor product. Also consider avoiding foods with additives that end in ...ates or ...ites.

Dr. Sherry Rogers in her book *Depression, Cured at Last* states, "Aspartame, known to consumers as Nutrasweet or Equal, (an artificial sugar substitute), is actually metabolized into methanol and formaldehyde. It causes depression and other malfunctions in the brain of humans to include, mood swings, mood changes, insomnia, mental retardation and seizures. There are numerous adverse effects of additives that are never mentioned. She goes on to say, "Any foods that have a yellow color (and shades of orange, green, or red) often contain the yellow dye tartrazine." It may not appear on the product label because some manufacturers are not legally obligated to include it. For example, if a baker used flour that contained yellow dye, making his product appear to have eggs in it, he does not have to include tartrazine on the label because *he* didn't add it to the flour, the company he bought the flour from, added it. Dr. Rogers says, "Tartrazine can lower zinc levels and in turn worsen brain conditions that are dependent upon normal zinc status, such as depression or hyperactivity. Always remember that all additives and colorings are mere chemicals that eventually further deplete the 'detox' nutrients that could have been utilized to make the brain's happy hormones. Food colorings are designed to fool the public into thinking the food is better than it is." Medication for a child dealing with neurotoxins means introducing a man made chemical into an already suppressed nervous system and may only mask the symptoms of his toxicity.

Basically, a daily diet should include vegetable proteins and whole grains, plenty of fresh fruits and vegetables and foods rich in tryptophan—turkey, fish, wheat germ, yogurt and eggs if one is not allergic or sensitive to these foods. Sugar should be avoided in all foods and in all its forms as much as possible. According to Nancy Appleton, Ph.D., author of *Lick The Sugar Habit,* "We humans need only two teaspoons of sugar in our body at any time in order to function properly. This amount can be obtained easily through the digestion of carbohydrates, protein and fats. Even if we were to eat no glucose or refined sugar at all, our bodies would still have plenty of sugar. Every extra teaspoon of refined sugar you eat works to throw the body out of balance and compromise its health."

Proteins are needed to balance blood sugar and keep ones energy level constant throughout the day. In *Natural Immunity: Insights on Diet and AIDS,* Noboru B. Muramoto says, "Grain eaters who chew well and avoid sugar have few problems. And if small amounts of beans, seeds, and vegetables are added to the grains, we can sustain health for a whole lifetime. The eating of good quality complex carbohydrates is an important factor in the development of the brain. These foods provide an even, steady supply of glucose for the brain's functioning."

Soy is a very beneficial plant protein, but we feel it is important to mention that only organically grown soy products should be used because commercially grown soy is one crop that is extensively sprayed with herbicides and pesticides. Also, peanuts and raisins have been identified as the most contaminated foods grown in America today. Consumers may want to consider eating only organic sources of these foods. In fact, we suggest that you consume organic foods as much as possible. *Diet For A Poisoned Planet: How To Choose Safe Foods For Your Family*, by David Steinman, gives the reader a deeper understanding of our research.

Food Sensitivities—Although some people have severe allergies to certain foods, almost everyone has food sensitivities. It is very true that one man's nutrition can be another man's poison, so individuality is extremely important when considering the family diet. The biggest offenders have been noted to be dairy products, wheat/gluten, corn, chocolate, sugar, citrus, food colorings, additives and flavor enhancers, such as MSG, and yeast which is not only present in baked goods, but also in orange juice, cheese, mushrooms (pure mold), pretzels and peanuts. Oranges (juice included) and dairy have been known to be responsible for ear infections.

Healthy Tips
- Fresh fruits and vegetables should be washed with a safe produce cleanser before consumption.

- Whole fruit is much better than juice because of the necessary fiber it provides. Fruit juice tends to hit the bloodstream faster, causing a dramatic change in ones blood sugar level.
- Fresh, uncooked foods provide live enzymes, which aid in digestion, leaving more energy for living!
- Basmati and brown rice have more fiber, more nutrients and are less refined than popular brand name rices.
- If sensitive or allergic to milk, consider a rice or soy substitute.
- For some people ice cream is one of the worst foods consumed today, (containing sugar, eggs; milk, additives and stabilizers) and should be a rare treat if consumed at all.
- Yellow cheeses, especially those available on the shelf, may be best left there as they consist of food coloring, preservatives and additives.
- A craving for chocolate may signify a magnesium deficiency, which according to Dr. Sherry Rogers, author and expert in health and nutrition, says is the beginning of all disease.
- Avoid all dyes/food colorings. Red dye in particular is known to pull zinc out of the body and brain. Zinc is essential for brain function and maintaining a healthy immune system.
- Butter can be a challenge for people who have a dairy sensitivity, canola or sunflower margarine might be a good alternative.
- Sugar pulls nutrients out of the body—especially calcium. If you want to have more calcium in your body, consider eating less sugar rather than drinking more milk.
- Chew food well; when food has not been thoroughly chewed it becomes putrefied in the stomach making it difficult for the body to absorb.
- Food digests better if beverages are consumed in larger quantities between meals, rather than with them.

- Spongy white bread that stays in a clump when squeezed will do the same in the bowels. Consider eating whole grain breads that break apart easily. Beware of any gluten sensitivity.
- For optimal nutrition choose fresh produce first, frozen second, and then canned.
- Use freshly ground peanut butter made from organic peanuts found in the refrigerated section or fresh organic in self-serve tubs.
- Try little known grains such as quinoa, millet, barley, kamut, rye, amaranth, or spelt.
- Always check for food sensitivities and a possible gluten sensitivity when considering which grains to consume.
- Ketchup is loaded with sugar, over-ripe tomatoes and food coloring, try an organic brand.

Today, so much of our diet depends upon taste and ease of preparation. We are definitely a fast food generation. Hopefully, this brief discussion has motivated you to think a little more deeply about the nutrition that goes into your body. After all, how can we expect health and well-being, sharp minds and enough energy if we don't work at nurturing each and every cell of our body with good nutrition.

Emotional Wellbeing—We mentioned that total nutrition is not just about food. Indeed, we also have our emotional wellbeing to look after. Here, we would like to mention some things that can be done to nurture our emotions as well as our physical bodies.

Exercise is a vital part of physical fitness as well as emotional health. Adults are not the only ones to experience stress and tension during the day, children do also. It is very important for them to be allowed time and space for various forms of exercise to alleviate this stress. We suggest they be taught some Brain Gym® exercises, such as Cross-Crawls and deep breathing exercises in order to help them relax during the day. In her book, *Smart Moves* Carla Hanaford, Ph.D. writes, "Brain Gym®

is a non-invasive common sense alternative to drug therapy. It effectively assists self-control training, motivation, self-esteem and anger management, natural neurotransmitter production (GABA) and Dopamine are stimulated when the whole brain is activated as it is with Brain Gym®. Hyperactive children and adults that I have worked with have been able—after doing the Brain Gym® activities—to slow and coordinate their movements, shift easily between details and the broad picture and focus on learning. With daily Brain Gym® the person gains more and more control as the frontal lobe and basal ganglion are being activated regularly and symptoms of ADHD lessen or completely disappear in an amazingly short time." At the Whole Child Institute we are familiar with Brain Gym®, exercises developed by Educational Kinesiologists Paul and Gail Dennison and suggest our clients do them routinely.

Colors and Sounds—Color and sounds affect us more than we probably know. We do know that colors like green and blue can be used effectively to produce a soothing atmosphere, and that colors like red and orange can excite and invigorate the senses. Dark, drab and dingy colors can inhibit optimism, inspiration, and therefore success. They encourage crime, inhibitions, inferiority complexes, and stunted development. If we use colors intelligently, we can provide an environment for our children that calms, cheers, and has the potential to inspire. Muscle testing using Kinesiology is a great way to show the power color has over us. This is mentioned in the book Diet Crime and Delinquency. Author Alexander Schauss states, "Evidence suggests that colors affect the body through the endocrine system. Specifically colors are seen by the eye. Through photoreceptors, colors effect the two master endocrine glands—the pineal and pituitary. In 1978, Dr. John Ott demonstrated to me the influence of the color pink on muscle strength." He goes on to describe how he was weak when looking at the color pink. He "suggested that corrections officials try to use a 'pink room' to curb physically violent inmates or delinquents. The U.S. Naval Correctional Center in

Seattle, Washington followed through with his suggestion. They were pleased to report that it worked quite well and that "since initiation of this procedure there have been no incidents of erratic or hostile behavior during the initial phase of confinement." Schauss adds, "...it is the experience of duty intake officers that the most likely outbursts of anger or violence occur when a new inmate is initially confined."

Sounds are important too. Many people find it exciting to think about the universe coming into being with the sound of the Creator's voice; "Let there be light," and there was light. We are all intensely affected by sounds around us whether they be soothing or harsh. It has been noted that children concentrate better on schoolwork when listening to classical music, such as Mozart, being played at a low volume in the same room. On the other hand, we all know the effects that loud advertising, traffic noise, and repeated irritating noises have on our nervous systems. It is a good bet that people who are obliged to listen to offensive sounds day after day will inevitably become sick, suffering from one of the innumerable nerve complaints which are the order of the day. For this reason we feel it is necessary for everyone to try to balance some soothing music or silence with the unavoidable noise of daily living. Listening to classical music while driving, doing housework, or helping a child with homework can be refreshing. Finally, we challenge our readers to turn off the radio and TV and suggest that those around them be still and quiet for a short time each day. One may find that silence is truly golden!

Dr. John Willard says, "Good health should not be thought of as the absence of disease. If we are in control of our health, disease will not take control." We hope this chapter helps our readers sort out the numerous puzzle pieces that make up total nutrition. Further information and resources dealing with nutrition are listed in Appendix IV-A.

Chapter Eleven

As a single mother of two challenging children, Peggy Specker knew she had her work cut out for her. Her search for a summer tutor led her to the Whole Child Institute where she learned healthy ways of dealing with their challenges. Her story starts with Missy, her first born.

"Missy was a very easy-going baby, happy and content. I could sit her almost anywhere and she was OK with what was going on. She had a lot of ear infections but half the time I didn't know she had them because she was so easy-going. I would take her in for her baby shots and it would be discovered upon exam. She was always given antibiotics for them.

As a toddler, Missy was typical and very social. We moved into a townhome and she knew the neighbors before I did! The one negative thing about Missy's behavior was that she was always slow. Her teachers also noticed that it took her forever to do something. It wasn't that she didn't understand what she was to do; she just dawdled instead of focusing on a task. Generally she avoided any kind of work, chores or school work, at all costs. When I took a college course in Occupational Therapy, some of the information I studied helped me to see that Missy probably was dealing with ADD. I had her evaluated by a doctor, but his idea of an evaluation was for me to check off some things on a form. Her score showed she was on the borderline. I didn't address the issue medically then, but tried changing her environment slightly. At school, her teacher and I worked out a plan to have her sit in a different area of the classroom where there were fewer distractions. She was allowed to wear earplugs in order to cut down on distracting noises.

When Missy was in third grade we tried Ritalin. It didn't seem to be working very well. She didn't like how she felt on it and the teacher didn't see any change in her behavior. Then in fourth grade we tried Dexedrine, which appeared to help Missy with staying on task. There was a big change in her school performance. She could sit still in her seat longer and concentrate on her work.

Dexedrine is an appetite suppressant, so while Missy was on it, her weight was tracked. She had always been tiny and petite; her doctor and I had already been following her growth curve for the last couple of years. I had a specialist do some tests for growth hormones and found out her body was not making enough of them. Her doctor prescribed artificial growth hormones and now she has been growing an inch every three months. Her insulin level was also low and they talked about possible thyroid problems. These are two areas that doctors usually check with these kids because they are typical problems for them. Medication is known for interfering with growth hormones and some ADD is actually caused by a thyroid imbalance that can be cleared up with natural substances.

I discovered the Whole Child Institute while searching for a tutoring program for Missy's younger brother, Scottie. I am a single mom working full-time, so I needed some good options for him for the summer. I wanted him to have some tutoring help so he wouldn't lose as much over the summer as he usually did. I felt that the summer school program offered at his school would be OK, but they had never offered to extend his Special Education, IEP (Individual Education Plan), services over the summer. I am going to push for that this year. What I have to do is convince the staff that he loses knowledge dramatically over the summertime when he doesn't have any follow-up. In Minnesota that is the only criteria that schools use to decide whether or not to establish an individual summer, special education, program.

In my search for a summer educator, I picked up various brochures including one about the Whole Child Institute. I went through all of the information I had accumulated and called around. I ended up deciding that starting with an assessment through the Whole Child Institute was where I should begin in order to get some help for Scottie. Missy came with us and I found many resources and solutions that were helpful for her too.

Scottie was a difficult baby. As an infant it seemed like he learned to scream the day he was circumcised and he's never stopped! He was always screaming and crying. He and Missy were total opposites. We had a mobile that was continuously moving and he would quickly get bored with that, but if **he** was moving, he was usually happy. I called him my 'colicky baby,' just because of all the crying he did. When he was a year old, he learned how to climb out of his crib. I would go to the laundry room while he was in his crib, come back, and he would be out running around. He was very strong. He was the kid at daycare, climbing on the jungle gym before anyone else his age. Physical activity has always been important for Scottie. He learned how to ride a bike at the age of three, without training wheels. I purchased a bike for him and left the training wheels on in order to prevent accidents. To date, T-ball and bike riding are the things he likes to do most.

Scottie also had difficulties falling asleep. I had to stay in his room and lay with him, or rub his back until he fell asleep. Some nights it took 10-15 minutes. Other nights it took up to an hour for him to fall asleep.

I knew Scottie was dealing with ADHD before he started school. In kindergarten, we didn't do anything about it, but I knew that by first grade I would need to intervene somehow.

In first grade, Scottie got detention the first or second week of school. He and another little boy, with similar problems, littered the bathrooms by stuffing toilet paper in all the toilets. First graders typically don't get detention, but he did. Shortly after that, he was diagnosed by a psychologist, as dealing with a Learning Disability and Attention Deficit Hyperactivity Disorder. I chose to put him on Ritalin. I never gave my kids any medication on the weekends or through the summers, but two years ago, it was apparent that Scottie's behavior was getting worse. I gave him medication on weekdays because I couldn't be there to help guide him through the day.

This year his doctor switched him to time-released Dexedrine. Unfortunately, he is medicated continually and he has been progressively getting worse. Through the Whole Child Assessment, I learned that Scottie might have a problem with heavy metals that will need to be cleansed from his system. Both children have some intense visual integration processing needs that I am looking at getting addressed. Missy and Scottie are excited about eventually getting off their medication by eating healthy, drinking lots of pure water, and attending to their environmental, structural, and nutritional needs. I am looking forward to working with the various resource people recommended by the Whole Child Institute in order to discover a healthier direction for my children."

Peggy is now a volunteer Occupational Therapist for the Whole Child Institute. She helps parents determine if their child needs Occupational Therapy and is familiar with Sensory Integration Processing.

Chapter Twelve

Terri Tulenchik changed her whole family's diet to a healthier one after witnessing a whole child assessment being done for her son Joey. We are very proud to share her story.

"My son, Joey, was born in 1991. He experienced respiratory distress at birth and he was diagnosed with pneumonia. He required intensive care, intravenous antibiotics, and nebulizing lung treatments. We continued therapy with him at home, medicating and pummeling him to keep his airway open.

Despite Joey's dramatic arrival, he became a thriving, breast-fed, baby and he doubled his birth weight in two months. Shortly thereafter he became chronically ill with colds and ear infections. He was frequently given antibiotics for these illnesses and sometimes as many as three different antibiotics were tried for a persistent infection because his body would either be resistant to the medication or he would be allergic to it. When he was on antibiotics he would get rashes, allergic reactions, diarrhea, constipation, and canker sores.

At two years of age, a more thorough assessment was indicated. Joey's development, at this point, was not only delayed but had regressed. His behaviors and mannerisms were totally bizarre and I would describe them as 'ballistic' in nature. Joey used to eat or try to eat non-food items. I caught him more than once trying to eat the bark off of trees, only to discover later, that he had a mineral deficiency. Emotionally, Joey had become completely withdrawn and eventually he was diagnosed with autism.

At three-and-a-half, Joey was diagnosed with encopresis, a condition in which the colon and gastro-intestinal tract become enlarged and stretched, making elimination extremely difficult.

He struggled with diarrhea while on antibiotics, and after the treatment he would become constipated and would not have a bowel movement for ten to fourteen days. Then it would be almost two weeks before he would go again, but only while wearing a diaper. This pattern soon developed into a serious bowel condition. As a two year old when asked to sit on the toilet he would scream. Eventually, as I rewarded him for his efforts, he learned to tolerate sitting on the toilet, but he still could not have a bowel movement there. I tried relaxation therapy which included calm, relaxing music, but nothing worked. He would sit there for thirty minutes to an hour with no results.

Joey struggled for nine months with mineral oil and over-the-counter laxatives suggested by his doctor, but they didn't work and Joey's colon was still not functioning properly. He would have involuntary diarrhea while he slept and if we added fiber to his diet, he would become constipated. He did not gain weight or grow in height at all during this time.

By the age of five, Joey had been in Early Childhood Special Education for three years. He was unmanageable and his unpredictable behaviors at school were of great concern to me. I chose to try Ritalin and his teacher noted that his vocabulary and his ability to converse had improved. He was also able to handle himself better during unstructured play time. Joey was no longer aggressive to the other children, but he continued to have unpredictable behavior and would easily become frustrated with his schoolwork.

Unfortunately, the side effects of Ritalin were horrendous for Joey. He began to show signs of Obsessive Compulsive Disorder. At this point Joey was always crabby. He would also grind his teeth, and exhibited garbled speech. He became resistant as well as downright belligerent. He couldn't eat or get to sleep at night, and sometimes was unable to stay awake in the afternoon, falling asleep in class. He developed rashes, belly aches, and canker sores. Sometimes a canker sore would involve at least two-thirds of his tongue and/or cheeks. At one point, he had an allergic reaction to the Ritalin; in which his throat and tongue swelled up becoming worse until he was hospitalized. The Ritalin depleted his immune system; he was found to have strep throat and mononucleosis. He was also suffering from dehydration.

Fortunately, I heard about a natural food substance, which helps in the detoxification of people dealing with ADD/ADHD. While attending a support group I had joined for parents with kids on Ritalin, I heard a talk on alternative treatments given by Allen Becker and received a brochure for the Whole Child Institute. I felt good about the information I received at the class and I chose to try a particular supplement the instructor spoke about.

The supplement arrived on Joey's fifth birthday; what a wonderful gift! The results have been absolutely life changing! After only eighteen days, Joey was able to have a bowel movement on the toilet! His body had been going through a cleansing cycle and he was having diarrhea. I sat him on the toilet for ninety minutes before he relaxed enough to allow it to happen. The whole time he cried out in pain. I sat with him and encouraged him to just let go and let it happen. When it did, we were excited. And was he proud! Each day he realized that he had done it before and that it was OK to do it again. In weeks, bowel movements that used to take an hour became a normal, everyday process. He no longer struggles with a bowel condition at all. It is completely normal in every way.

After our visit with the Whole Child Institute staff, we modified Joey's diet. On Easter morning he found a basket full of fruit. We eliminated refined sugars and began using purified water. We noticed improvements at school the second week of his diet. Each morning at his school, he shares something of interest and he has read a book to his entire class. He comes home from school singing nursery rhymes and sharing information about his day. He is bright-eyed and bushy-tailed. He can swing now and pumps his legs without help. He spends less time in obsessive/compulsive behaviors and frequently asks to be read to. Joey loves to play with his sister and enjoys doing handstands with her on the couch. He likes to count the groceries when I bring them into the house. His coloring has improved and he colors objects now rather than the whole page. He has learned a computer program that he enjoys very much and we had the program installed on our computer for him. Our whole family was impressed with what Joey could do on the computer. His eye-hand coordination was perfect. He had absolutely no difficulties and it was a great boost to his self-confidence.

His immune system has been restored. I have been able to eliminate all over-the-counter medications for colds, flu, allergies, and/or canker sores. Joey's health is excellent! He is happy and has a great sense of humor. He uses and shows his emotions. He can eat without biting himself, and is getting better at using utensils. Since we started his nutritional program eleven months ago, he has grown four inches, gained seven pounds, and no longer rocks himself to sleep.

Joey now attends school and is completely drug-free. He can play with his friends and siblings, and for the first time in his life, he gets excited about presents and parties. He asks questions and understands instructions. He can communicate and express himself well. He loves music and knows many songs. His fine motor skills have greatly improved. He can now use scissors, glue and tape. He traces his name as well as letters and numbers. He is willing to wash, groom and dress himself. It no longer hurts him when I wash his hair or clip his nails. This shows that his sensory integration processing has improved.

It is no longer a struggle to take him out into the community. Joey participates in sports, is eager to learn, and has become even more independent. I believe the personal connections I've made that led me to the Whole Child Institute were answers to prayer. It is truly amazing and I am forever grateful for the Whole Child Institute."

As a result of her experience with her son, Joey, Terri Tulenchik reaches out to educate families and teachers in her small town in Northwestern Minnesota. Her story has caught the attention of Joey's school officials and has touched many lives in her community.

Chapter Thirteen

Stephanie's mother had worked at a petroleum refinery while she was pregnant; she had also placed Stephanie in a daycare facility close to the plant so she could nurse her. Little did she know how toxic and obstinate her child would become as a result of being so close to the refinery. Stephanie eventually needed homeopathic petroleum in order to counteract her high level of toxicity, which at one point was only masked by the use of Ritalin. Her mother starts at the beginning.

"Stephanie was the most wonderful baby in the world. At ten days old, she started sleeping through the night; but when she reached age two, she went totally ballistic. She fought every request. She was the most obstinate kid in the world. Potty training was very difficult.

I began to worry about my temper and my abusive reactions to her obstinance. My husband noticed how out of control I was getting. We worked out a signal, where he would squeeze my shoulder to let me know when I needed to calm down. This kept Stephanie from getting the idea that her father was on her side. It also worked wonders for me because I felt his concern and support.

Preschool and kindergarten became my time for respite. Stephanie had a teacher who liked her and accepted her in spite of her shortcomings, but she did not develop the friendships one would expect. This continued to puzzle me until about eight years later, when I attended a Twin Cities Autism Society Conference and began to realize Stephanie was probably dealing with High Functioning Autism.

Stephanie's pediatrician referred her to a psychologist. Stephanie tested very high in reading comprehension and vocabulary. The test results showed that Stephanie, who had just finished first grade, was reading several grade levels ahead. The psychologist felt she had signs of ADHD (Attention Deficit Hyperactivity Disorder) yet felt she did not require medication at that time.

When Stephanie was in second grade I heard about Ritalin and its 'magical' effects at a ChADD (Children and Adults with Attention Deficit Disorder) sponsored seminar. I was so exhausted from dealing with Stephanie that I went back to her pediatrician and begged to have her put on Ritalin. Our pediatrician felt that Stephanie was not hyperactive, but she agreed to write a prescription. We started her on Ritalin late that summer.

Stephanie was on Ritalin for eighteen months. During that time she had dramatic highs and lows. Our lives revolved around her Ritalin schedule. If she was going to her ice skating class, I would have to make sure that her Ritalin was working at that time. If she was experiencing a 'low' time, she would just lay on the ice, eat ice shavings, and play with her skates. She would do anything but skate.

As the Ritalin began to kick in she would experience some sense of normality. She was able to listen to her teacher, be attentive, and was actually able to focus. It was only during the 'high times' that the medication did what is it was intended to do.

As the Ritalin began to wear off, Stephanie would become lethargic. She would grab on to me and would cling to me saying things like, 'I love you Mom, I'm sorry, I don't mean it'. 'I'm sorry!' During these 'low times,' she would just sit in a corner and read, read, read. She would communicate, but it was like she was in another world. If I told her to do something, she would do it, but she was more like a zombie than a child. That wasn't my little girl. She also lost her sense of humor during the 'low times.' She was so serious and worried about everything. It was like she was drugged, and she was.

Eventually, I decided I could not leave her on the Ritalin. It had given me a reprieve from her very difficult behavior, and I had some time to collect my thoughts, but now I had to get back to dealing with the real problem.

I discontinued the Ritalin. At first, it was like she still the drug in her. For about two months she was quite easy to deal with. I thought, this was the child that I had been looking for all this time. After those two months, the drug was completely out of her system and she was back to 'bouncing off the walls,' obstinate, inattentive, and talking back. She would argue every point, and she had an excuse for everything.

I heard about the Whole Child Institute through a friend. I was thrilled to find other parents who understood what I was dealing with. I am forever grateful for their support and guidance. They helped me connect with a doctor of preventive medicine. Eventually, that doctor discovered that Stephanie, her younger sister, and I, were dealing with petroleum sensitivities as a result of my work in the refinery.

When Stephanie is riding in the car in the city and we are in a lot of stop and go traffic, she starts to get very nervous and gets headaches. I no longer let her ride the bus to school, because I noticed that if she was fine at home in the morning, but rode the bus to school, she would be disruptive in class. If I drove her to school, that didn't happen, so her doctor and I figured out it was the fumes from the bus that were bothering her.

I pulled Stephanie out of school halfway through third grade and sent her to the Whole Child Institute for Learning Gap Therapy and their homeschool program. She was so used to being able to walk around and be this spaced out kid with no accountability. The learning specialist worked with her on thinking skills, processing what she was told, social skills, and what others expected.

During the summer I worked on cleaning up her diet and trying to get her detoxified.

By fourth grade, she had been off the Ritalin for several months and was eating a much healthier diet. I started her on a natural food supplement two weeks before school started. She was holding her own and she was doing very well. She started fourth grade at a private religious school that has a special education department. After some diagnostic testing, it was apparent that Stephanie had Dyslexia in both Math and Reading. I was surprised because Stephanie reads everything she gets a hold of and understands it all. Academically, fourth grade was difficult for her because we were still in the process of discovering her learning style, and her social behavior was still a big problem.

Stephanie would become totally overwhelmed when given a full page of multiplication or addition problems. It would 'freak her out' and she would just shut down mentally. At those times, she couldn't do spelling, penmanship, or even reading which is what she's really good at. Her first report card was not good, she had one F and the rest were all C's and D's, although she did get an A- in reading. The problem was not that she couldn't do the work, but she wouldn't get assignments done. I spoke with Stephanie's teacher and she modified her assignments and had her do smaller amounts of math at a time. Instead of having her write out spelling words in the evenings, she would spell them for me orally. The next report card placed her on the 'A' honor roll.

While working with the staff at the Whole Child Institute I learned to be a good advocate for my child. At one point I noticed there was a problem with Stephanie's math, I told her teacher, 'This math isn't working, let's try it another way.' I asked that Stephanie's writing assignments be cut back because she has an output disability. ADD and ADHD are *output* processing disabilities in which children have difficulty staying on task and getting the manual work done, whereas a learning disability is an *input* processing disability in which children have difficulty understanding what they are being taught.

Once the year got rolling, the principal suggested that I set up a weekly meeting with the classroom teacher, the Special Ed teacher and herself to talk about Stephanie and make sure that we were meeting her needs. The classroom teacher was a little hard to convince, but eventually she understood that Stephanie is a special needs child and can't just be lumped in with everyone else. For example, when they would have treats at school, it was important that Stephanie not get any wheat or dairy. About halfway through the year Stephanie's doctor told us that she should be able to try wheat and dairy again. One day at school, she had a pizza that had dairy and wheat in it. Her teacher told me, 'This really is not working, because she just gets out of control on days when she eats anything with wheat.' 'I can tell when she's had it.' She then proceeded to tell me that on days Stephanie had food that she was sensitive to she would not listen, she was up and down out of her seat, she would sharpen her pencil five times a day, and go to the restroom eight times a day. She was very disruptive in class, inattentive, and hyperactive.

I was delighted that the teacher finally understood Stephanie's food sensitivities. At the beginning of the school year she had not even been willing to change any class treats to something Stephanie could have. A few simple changes in her cookie recipes would have done the trick.

The summer between Stephanie's fourth and fifth grade we started building a new home and really messed up our diets. It became very obvious that eating healthy was just as important for me as it was for my girls. Most of our time was spent working on our property, clearing our land every evening, and consequently eating a lot of restaurant food. We felt the effects of that up to six months later! I can see an improved difference in all of us now that we are settled into our new home.

With the new house, we are also living in toxins that are working their way out of the carpet padding and building materials. It's very expensive to get carpets outgassed, and at the time we built there was no place to get carpets outgassed *before* they were installed. To have the carpet outgassed once it was installed cost us about $2,400.00 for our home, which is not that big. They use vegetable based cleaning products, and they said it would be like cleaning our carpet ten times in one day. It gets all the gasses out. They measure the gasses coming out of the carpet beforehand and again afterwards to make sure the gasses are all out. The average carpet padding is made of petroleum products, glues, etc. however, you can find padding that is safe. This is usually padding with no colored pieces in it.

My entire childhood tells me that I have had ADD all my life. I remember doing things that were so stupid and awful and later, thinking, 'Why did I do that?' It didn't occur to me that I had ADD until I started going through this with Stephanie. Then, I pressured myself more than anyone else to get help for her because of my experience with ADD and what happens to you socially. I was 38 years old when I realized I didn't have a friend from my childhood or high school years. When you don't develop good social skills, you just kind of blast everybody away. I saw all the social problems that Stephanie had and I didn't want that to happen to her. It wasn't so much that Stephanie was hyperactive, it was her oppositional defiant behavior that made life with her so miserable. Working one-on-one with the learning specialist at the Whole Child Institute helped a lot.

Our family life has improved since I have learned how to deal with Stephanie. Keeping her on a healthy diet is of major importance so she can hear me when I'm talking to her. Once I saw what exposure to different foods, like chocolate and ice cream would do to her, I was encouraged to help her stay away from the foods she was sensitive to. At first it was difficult to see which foods were affecting her. Once I cleaned up her diet, taking out foods she was sensitive to and introducing healthier foods, she became a clean pool of clear water. If she ate an offending food it was like dumping a cup of muddy water into her. Wow! Could we ever notice the difference. This was very helpful and, in my eyes, it gave the Whole Child Institute all the credibility in the world. Stephanie is very good about her diet. She knows what she can and cannot eat, because we taught her early. I can't imagine having a teenager and suddenly telling them they can't have milk, ice cream, or chocolate because it affects their behavior.

At eleven years old, Stephanie's major challenge is her social problems. She has changed schools a lot. Making friends is very easy for Stephanie, keeping them is difficult. She needs to learn how to keep a friend.

I am grateful for what I have gained from the Whole Child Institute. I found the emotional support I needed as well as new resources to explore. Many people seek my advice now, because they know what I have been through. They don't want to spend the kind of money I did when I first started looking for help for Stephanie. I refer them to the Whole Child Institute. The specialists at the Whole Child Institute know which resources work, and what doctors you can trust, so parents don't have to try a number of different places and spend a lot of money unnecessarily."

Stephanie's mother was one of the first parents to begin working with us. We began to call her our 'guinea pig' mom. She still refers to herself that way. As we discovered less costly, less invasive, and more effective resources she would try them out. She has blazed a wonderful trail for other parents to benefit from.

Chapter Fourteen

Evan was just turning ten when he was rescued by the Whole Child Institute. His maturational age seemed more like age six. He had been placed in an autism program where he would roll on the floor unable to cooperate with the academic regimes of his class. He was rewarded with chocolate candy bars for "good behavior," which only caused him to lose bowel control at school. Like many other parents, his mother brought him to the Whole Child Institute feeling frustrated and confused. Here is her story...

"Before I found out about the Whole Child Institute my eldest son, Evan, was diagnosed with ADHD and Asperger's Syndrome (a form of autism). Evan seemed to be a normal infant and toddler, but went through some hard times with our family. My husband and I separated when Evan was two-and-a-half and his younger brother, Tom, was only six months old. We had been living in Oregon, when I left my husband, and moved to Minnesota with our two boys. Six months later my husband came to Minnesota for a visit with the boys. He told me they would all be staying with his mother in Southern Minnesota. Approximately two to three days later my sister in-law called to tell me that he had taken the boys to Alaska because he wanted full custody. In a panic I called legal services provided by my county. They advised me that there was nothing I could do because we were not divorced or even legally seperated.

Several months after the boys left with their father, he called me and said that Evan was having some problems. He told me that he was unable to feed himself without using two hands in order to bring a spoon to his mouth. A year later he put Evan into a special education program. Two to three years after the boys had been taken by their father, he called and told me that the boys had been taken into state custody and he was being charged with abuse and neglect. With financial help from my mother, I hired a lawyer and went up to Alaska in order to regain custody of my children. I won the case and brought the boys home to live with me.

My boys were a wreck. They were totally disoriented and out of control. We had to get reacquainted and I needed to figure out how to be a mom again. I brought them home in July and Evan started kindergarten in September. From the beginning, he had trouble being in school. He would spin and hum and was unable to listen and sit still. His teacher recommended that I have him assessed for ADHD. I waited until the next school year thinking that maybe he would mature. During the first month of the following school year, Evan's new teacher also suggested that I have him assessed for ADHD. I did and he was put on Ritalin. It helped him a little bit but the improvements did not last.

The following year in second grade, I put him into a new school. I sent him to school without the Ritalin hoping that he could handle it. It was a disaster, he couldn't. He hummed, he spun, and he would not stay in his chair or do any of his school work. The doctor I was working with tried Dexedrine, then Ritalin again—this time a long lasting form. Evan still wasn't able to get his school work done.

In third grade Evan couldn't do anything, even on the drugs. I took him to a child psychiatrist who diagnosed him with Asperger's Syndrome. The psychologist at his school recommended I have him assessed for the Autism program at a special school where he would have an aide working with him. When he was switched to this school his medication was also changed. He was put on Adderal, a different kind of Dexedrine. Evan was doing all right in school, but at home when he was coming down off his medication, he was a 'basket case.' He would cry and scream and be impossible to reason with. He also talked about how he hated his life and wished he would die. He was sick to his stomach and would throw up on the school bus just after taking his pills in the morning. This happened about once every two weeks. He also lacked an appetite and it was difficult to get him to eat.

At the end of that year I was desperate. My aunt, who was a distributor for a nutritional supplement containing nutritious algae, recommended that I try Evan on some. I worked with my doctor and took him off his Dexedrine. I sent him to school that fall off of medication. He was actually able to sit in class and not cause a disruption, yet he was still unable to do the work and was caught in some bad behavior patterns, which I feel were promoted by his autism program and his instructors. At school Evan was being treated as if he was special and needed coddling. No one tried to 'set him straight' when he pulled his negative behavior. Often they would bribe him with rewards of candy and pop in order to motivate him to get his work done. As I look back I can see how the candy and pop only added to his physical and emotional problems. He was even having bowel movements in his pants while at school. At home it was a struggle getting him to do his homework. The school staff began pushing me to put him back on drugs. I refused!

Desperate to find an alternative, I searched around for help. One day, in my brother's chiropractic office, I was looking at a magazine with a story about the Whole Child Institute. I immediately called to set up a Whole Child Assessment. The assessment helped me see that Evan might be suffering from a toxicity problem and that he was a severe patterned learner with an out-put disability. After the assessment I saw a health care professional about getting him on a detoxifying program. I began feeding him only organically grown foods—no red meats, lots of filtered water, and took dairy and wheat products from his diet. He also began taking vitamin and mineral supplements.

Through Evan's assessment, I learned that Evan was a right brain learner. Most school systems are set up to accommodate left brain learners; right brain learners do not learn well in such a system. The Whole Child Institute helped me explore some alternatives such as the Kumon Math and Reading program.

Evan was invited to take part in the educational pilot program at the Whole Child Institute. I withdrew Evan from his autism program in order to homeschool him. He received special education at the Whole Child Institute as part of his homeschooling.

The homeschool program at the Whole Child Institute included cutting edge therapies that aided Evan in his developmental progress. My son had a severe disconnection between his body and his brain. Techniques were incorporated in order to help him develop a better body/brain connection. He tended to space out and go into his own little world. At these times it was difficult to have a conversation with him. He wouldn't respond when someone was talking to him. His spatial awareness, his ability to know where his body was in space, was very low. His maturational age was that of a six year old when he started the program, yet he was about to celebrate his tenth birthday.

After one month I had already noticed improvements in Evan's behavior and a new willingness to learn. When I asked him to do something he would respond immediately. One day I asked Evan to feed the cats. Normally he would have ignored me or argued about it and not done it at all. This time he simply went and did it. What a pleasant surprise! He also stopped spacing out and was able to respond immediately when being talked to. He became more positive and less confused.

Socially, Evan usually went through hell with my two year old nephew Timmy. Timmy would zero in on him and harass him knowing that Evan would 'freak' if he came near him. Recently I had gone to my mother's with Evan. Timmy was there and went directly for Evan to try and get a reaction from him. My mom and sisters told him to leave Evan alone. Surprisingly, Evan calmly looked at them and said, ' Oh, that's all right; he's just a baby.'

I am also seeing Evan exhibit some new social abilities, which he previously had lacked. He never really liked to be touched; now he is more approachable and he is more able to receive affection. One day some kids came to play with Evan's brother Tom. Evan let them play with his toys, even his legos, which is something that never would have happened before. One day I took him to see his brother's hockey game. He usually hates to go. This time he actually watched the game and interacted with me, making comments about the game.

Evan is learning the basics in math and reading, something he wasn't getting in school. He also was showing some dyslexic tendencies. The educational specialist at the Whole Child Institute taught me how to address this problem. I have recently had Evan read to me and was pleasantly surprised to find that he was reading better than I had ever heard him read before. He could flow with the text and even add inflexion for the emotional content. He never once reversed his words or skipped words as he used to do. In school they just wanted to push him through to the next grade even though they felt he wasn't ready.

Our home life has changed dramatically thanks to the Whole Child Institute. Evan's brother Tom has also started to calm down and is behaving better. This was a benefit I never saw coming. I don't feel like every day is a struggle with my children and we all live a more peaceful life.

I believe that our society has to implement new programs in order to address the growing number of children with learning and behavioral difficulties. I have seen that these learning difficulties are being promoted by poor quality food, produced by the use of deadly chemicals, which pollute our environment and our bodies."

After only three months of working with the Whole Child Institute, Evan acted at least two years older than when he started. His self-worth rose daily and he became excited about teaching other children, including his younger brother, how to think, process, and read without symptoms of dyslexia. He is working through a detoxification program which is relieving his symptoms of autism. The psychotherapy he receives at the Institute helps him to heal from his confusing and abusive past.

Evan, Camye and her little sister Marissa were one of the first children to go through the Whole Child Institute's pilot program. During the first month they learned to manage their behavior and worked on body/brain connections. The second month focused on academic basics in math and reading, as well as learning their own phone numbers, addresses, etc. The third month involved peer mentoring, teaching what they had learned to new students as they entered the program. Dyslexic symptoms disappeared, reading and math skills drastically improved, and best of all, behavior was at its finest.

Chapter Fifteen

Tony had many emotional problems when we began to work with him. He seemed depressed, and it was as if he was trapped inside of himself. He is intelligent, yet could not retain anything. Sadly, he seemed to have given up on himself. Our educational specialist found that using praise only interrupted his thought process. She pointed this out to his mother and she changed the way she interacted with him. More specific encouragement allowed him to praise himself and his self-confidence took off. Here is Tony's story as described by his mother.

"Tony was a very good baby. He ate well and was a good sleeper. Once he could get around, he always seemed to need me nearby. He needed me even more when he became a toddler. His temperament became nasty and demanding; this behavior continued to escalate until he never wanted to play alone. It became a major challenge for both of us.

Tony seemed to be behind his peers in understanding things like colors, the alphabet, and various cognitive concepts. We tried to have him take some pre-kindergarten tests, but he would not cooperate at all. We went back after six months and an Early Childhood Special Education (ECSE) teacher was asked to observe him. Again, he would not attempt any of the tasks. The ECSE teacher set up an Early Childhood Special Education screening to determine his functional level. This time the screening began at a developmental level Tony was comfortable with and he was quite cooperative. His test scores helped to qualify him for Early Childhood Special Education services. He spent two years in an ECSE program before we sent him to kindergarten at age six.

Kindergarten was a disaster. He gravitated towards the kids

with behavior problems. When his class had story time he would roll on the floor and not pay attention. I felt I could not get the teacher to understand what he needed. Tony became depressed and frustrated.

When Tony had finished his very dismal year of kindergarten, I was determined to find out why everything came so slowly to him. I found out about the Whole Child Institute from Learning Disabilities of Minnesota. I took him for a Whole Child Assessment and received a great deal of helpful information. During the assessment Tony showed an interest in learning. Since he was completely resistant to working with me, I thought I would try having him work with someone at the Institute.

Their educational specialist helped Tony realize that he can learn if he works hard. She worked closely with him in the summertime after kindergarten and then I enrolled him in Kumon Math.

When I saw signs of Tony wanting to learn I realized that the work the specialist was doing with him was very important. She was able to get him processing information. His daily work from the Kumon center allowed him to begin developing his attention skills. Although he still has to work on his ability to focus on a task, Tony and I have both realized that he can learn, and it has done so much to raise his level of self-confidence."

When Tony would ask his Kumon instructor a question, she would answer him 'with a question' in order to encourage him to figure things out for himself. In just a few days, he was able to process information and work independently. With each passing day he was able to successfully do another learning task and would beam as he showed off for his mother.

Chapter Sixteen

**Instilling the Love of Learning and the Self-Taught Child—
The Kumon Philosophy:** *"Kumon really helps me do better at
school. I usually finish my tests before the other kids and that's
fun because I get to help my teacher."*

—Jennifer Werner, MN fourth grader

The Whole Child Institute introduces parents and educators
to a unique educational service, which can follow a student
from setting to setting, be it home, school, corrections, etc. This
service can be used for remedial, on-going, or accelerated
educational needs.

Since 1958, Kumon Math and Reading Centers have helped
more than 8 million students in 30 countries build the
confidence they need to succeed in school as well as in an
increasingly competitive world. Kumon is now the largest
supplemental education service in the world and is dedicated to
helping children excel in math and reading while gaining a love
for learning.

Toru Kumon's method is rooted in the belief that everyone
possesses unlimited potential along with an innate desire and
capacity to learn. Once spared the anxiety of keeping up with
others, we can all make dramatic progress.

Kumon takes students back to the basics and teaches
independent learning skills. Since Kumon students work
independently, they are able to see their own progress and to
take pride in their growing success. The self-confidence, time
management skills, study habits, and self-discipline that
students gain through Kumon will extend beyond their formal

education and benefit them in everything they do. The results can last a lifetime!

Kumon's success relies on five key points...

- An individualized program
- Repetition
- An easy starting point to build confidence
- Self-learning
- Good study habits

Kumon's approach to learning is one that requires daily practice and the belief that a moderate amount of regular study is more valuable and more effective than intensive, but irregular study.

Students begin Kumon at a familiar level allowing them to complete a pre-determined number of problems quickly and easily. This results in increased confidence and allows the student to experience success right from the start.

In Kumon, each student advances at his or her own pace according to individual ability rather than by age or grade level. To do this, Kumon presents math and reading concepts in a highly sequential manner, providing ample practice for each step. The math program moves students from learning to count to integral calculus. The reading series builds comprehension and analytical skills.

Students gradually advance through each level, practicing daily and reworking incorrect problems until a perfect score is achieved on each worksheet.

This process of supervised self-learning, the truly unique aspect of the Kumon method, gives students a sense of pride in their own achievement. Along with the Kumon Instructor a variety of people can be responsible for facilitating the learning; parents, teachers, behavior technicians, and relatives are some of the people who can oversee the success of each student.

The Kumon system emphasizes self-learning with a unique set of materials, which each student completes on their own, and ultimately supervised by a trained Kumon instructor. Math concepts within the system are sequentially organized so they are easy to follow as they gradually increase in difficulty. The materials are designed to provide a student with the necessary practice of math skills, which promote speed and accuracy while building a thorough understanding of mathematical concepts. The Kumon Reading program uses independent learning materials, again supervised by a Kumon instructor. The materials present reading fundamentals in a step-by-step process which begins with word structure and progresses through sentence building, paragraph construction, passage analysis/summary and then critique. Phonics, spelling, traditional grammar, syntax and vocabulary building are all addressed in sequential worksheets. The focus of the reading program is the development of strong reading comprehension skills. Additionally, students learn about other subjects such as art and science as they read and respond to story selections.

Located in schools, community centers, churches, and shopping centers, Kumon Centers are literally right next door to playgrounds and football fields—in the heart of neighborhoods around the world.

Observers of Kumon Centers are often overwhelmed by several factors:

- **Student concentration and attentiveness**
- **Desire to attain new levels of performance**
- **Clear and measurable progress**
- **Cordial and team-like relationship between parents, instructor, and students.**
- **Young people who are as interested in math and reading as they are in other after school activities: sports, music, dance, gymnastics, Karate, etc.**

Based on the concept that self-directed study will develop initiative, independent work habits, and the ability to think and solve problems, a partnership between Kumon instructors, students, parents and classroom teachers is essential to a student's progress. The remarkable success of a Kumon student depends on it.

The Kumon Philosophy: Kumon is based on the philosophy that any child can succeed in mathematics or language study if it is presented in small, understandable segments, and if mastery is assured at each level before proceeding to the next level. Kumon can be expressed in six organizing principles...

Articulated learning that leads directly to calculus—The Kumon method is designed to help students of all ages and abilities achieve competency in higher level math and language study. Each Kumon level builds upon concepts mastered in previous levels in order to prepare students for higher level study.

Proper placement of the student—Each new Kumon student is given a placement test in order to accurately measure their mastery level. Students begin at a level that ensures immediate success to give them the confidence and motivation they need.

Repetition geared towards increased speed and accuracy— Kumon is not a "drill and kill" method of learning. The Kumon method is built upon the idea that repetition allows a student to master the work. This is essential to self-learning and to building self-confidence.

A stress free environment—Pressure from a classroom or group environment often dissuades students from trying harder in school. Kumon insists that its instructors act as *mentors or coaches*. Encouragement, not discouragement, is the motto for both instructors and parents; students are treated as individuals.

A strong family support system: *including oversight, correction, and encouragement*—Too often, parents are disengaged from their child's education. Kumon works expressly to engage or re-engage parents.

Independent learning—The best students are usually independent learners. This is essential to both academic success and success in life. The Kumon system was designed to produce independent learners who will be able to solve difficult problems and master difficult concepts regardless of the subject matter.

- **Kumon is an individualized system of learning for students of all ages and abilities.**

- **Kumon does not replace schools, it supplements them, and is surprisingly affordable.**

The Kumon Method

Students are given a placement test and then assigned materials that are deliberately easy. The comfortable starting point is essential to a student's long-term progress. Immediate success provides the confidence and motivation for a student to advance to more challenging materials. The materials are organized into carefully sequenced skill levels that range from preschool counting through college calculus. Kumon believes that children advance in mathematics at their own pace and according to individual ability rather than age. Students practice and rework incorrect problems to attain a score of 100% accuracy. Mr. Toru Kumon explained the philosophy behind the Kumon methodology, "The joy of receiving 100% not only assures subject knowledge, but also gives the student the confidence and motivation to continue to the next study level."

"While the worksheets do the teaching, Kumon instructors help their students to become self-learners."

—Linda Vettrus

Before students move onto the next concept and the next set of materials they must master each level which gradually increases in difficulty. Mastery of each concept provides the foundation necessary for applying the skill at more advanced levels. The typical Kumon student visits their local Kumon Center twice a week after school or work. There are no lectures and no direct instruction. Each student works independently on their own individual assignments and at a pace that is comfortable for them. Kumon staff are available to coach students as needed, usually to work with preschool children or when a new concept is introduced.

Just look at some of the success stories:

Richard Hoshino, a Kumon student for 15 years, recently took a silver medal at the International Math Olympiad and received the top scholarship for a first-year student at the University of Waterloo.

Susan Lee, of Phoenix, Arizona, scored a perfect 1600 on the SAT and has plans to attend an Ivy League school.

Kyoko Ina, U.S. pair figure skating olympian, completed the entire Kumon math program in the fourth grade (level O was the highest level at that time.)

These are just a few of the more than 10 million success stories that Kumon has produced.

"The best thing about Kumon is that it truly is surprisingly affordable.
                                        —Sally Jones, Kumon Parent

Instilling The Love of Learning

Co-author Linda Vettrus is a Kumon Math & Reading Franchise owner in Minnesota. The following is a testimony from one of Linda's own Kumon parents, Mr. John Werner. His daughter, Jennifer, provided the quote that began this chapter.

Dec. 18, 1996

Dear Linda,

I would like to thank you for the wonderful job you've done with my daughter, Jennifer. I first discovered the Kumon Math program from my brother. Both my nephew and niece are enrolled in a Kumon Center and are so excited by the results they have achieved. They boast that they are far ahead of the other kids in their class and now find math both fun and easy. With that kind of an endorsement I just had to enroll Jennifer. That was by far one of the best decisions I've made for Jennifer. Her overall attitude and self-esteem have skyrocketed since she started Kumon. She now has the confidence she needed.

Once Jennifer completed Level A Math, she could tell that Kumon was really helping her at school. She now tells me that, at school, she's always one of the first kids to get her math tests done and does so with very high accuracy. Both the speed and accuracy are attributed to the Kumon program. Because she finishes first, her teacher has her correct the tests of the other kids in her class.

I would also like to thank you Linda, as a Special Education teacher, for taking the extra time to informally test Jennifer for her vision skills. Your findings indicated a need for further testing and possibly some vision therapy. I followed your recommendations and had her evaluated by a behavioral optometrist who found that Jennifer had a vision tracking problem that could be corrected with reading glasses. Jennifer had complained for several years about headaches, fatigue, and frustration while reading or looking at the chalkboard in her classroom at school. After taking Jennifer to three different opticians who said she had no problems, I can't begin to tell you how relieved I was that the behavioral optometrist you recommended found her eye problem and knew of a simple technique to correct it.

After Jennifer was tested for vision therapy, the behavioral optometrist recommended several sessions, which helped Jennifer with her reading and comprehension skills. When I discovered that Kumon Math helped to increase a child's overall academics by 30% and that when taking the math and reading together, it increased by more than 75%, I couldn't resist enrolling Jennifer in the Kumon Reading program as well. I believe, had these problems not been discovered and corrected, educators would have told me she had Attention Deficit Disorder (ADD) and might have suggested some remedial program or drug treatment. I wonder how many kids could be helped by this therapy and the Kumon Math and Reading program, instead of struggling through school not to mention life in general. It's frustrating knowing that the present system just pushes young students ahead whether or not they have actually mastered the fundamental skills needed to figure out complex math problems which they will be facing in the future.

My daughter Jennifer took a break from her Kumon studies and one month later she told me, "Dad, I need to go back to Kumon, I really slipped in math this month at school".

I know I can count on Jennifer's progress through the Kumon Math and Reading program and look forward to seeing Jennifer become a truly independent self-learner.

Thanks again,

John Werner

Kumon is a proven method for all ages and abilities:

- *Gifted learners* who need to be challenged.

- *Average learners* who want or need to master current work.

- *Struggling learners* who need to review and learn at their own pace.

Information about Kumon Math and Language Programs...

Kumon USA, Inc.
North American Headquarters
Glenpointe Centre East, Second Floor
300 Frank W. Burr Boulevard
Teaneck, New Jersey 07666
Telephone: (201) 928-0444

Regional Info. Lines: 1·800·ABC·MATH

Website: http://www.kumon.com

A book entitled, *Every Child An Achiever: A Parent's Guide To The Kumon Method*, by David W. Russell, an investigative journalist who thoroughly researched the Kumon Method, is available at your local Kumon Center or can be ordered by calling 1-800-YES-Math.

Another book of interest to our readers might be *Positive Involvement: How to Teach Your Child Habits for School Success*, by Jack and Marsha Youngblood; available through Brown Wood Press: 1-800-283-1087.

Chapter Seventeen

Margaret was very angry and frustrated when she brought her daughter, Karen to us. These emotions stemmed from feeling out of control with her daughter's health and education. She was angry that the school seemed to have little help or hope for her daughter. She knew Karen was more intelligent than her work at school revealed to her teachers and that Karen's assets had gone unnoticed. She tells how her search for help led her to the Whole Child Institute and how she gained control over her daughter's health and education.

"Karen was a very easy baby. She always seemed happy and was easy to please. She did have some ear infections, but not more than most children get. As a toddler, she was outgoing and very much a leader. At about age three-and-a-half she changed and became more passive and unsure of herself. For instance, at her preschool screening for entering kindergarten, she was asked to write her name and when the examiner looked away, she slipped her paper and pencil onto the floor. Finally, her twin sister picked up her paper and wrote her name for her. I think that was my first clue that she was becoming less confident in her own abilities.

According to her first grade teacher, Karen was doing fine that year. However, in January, her class got a new teacher. This teacher noticed that Karen was not keeping up, so the following summer I had her tutored. Over the next two years I made a point of keeping in close contact with her teachers regarding her progress. I felt it was very important to do this in order to maintain a good relationship with her teachers. This also gave me more information as to how Karen was being taught.

Karen had just finished third grade when I found out about the Whole Child Institute. She had not been testing well in school, her reading comprehension was low and her teacher felt she wasn't grasping place values in math. I had her evaluated at school, but she did not qualify for Special Education. The school psychologist gave me a packet of information about ADD and said that at some point in her schooling Karen would qualify for Special Education. I left feeling angry and frustrated because I had not received any tangible solutions.

I called Karen's pediatrician to get some help, but he said there was nothing he could do unless I wanted to put Karen on drugs. Personally, he was against it, and believes they are overused. I was committed to *not* using Ritalin. Although I knew little about ADD, I did realize that there was no single answer to the problem.

Anxious to get answers and start helping Karen as quickly as possible, I investigated ADD more thoroughly. I went to a community education class on ADD where they handed out a brochure for the Whole Child Institute. The brochure mentioned Kumon Math, which I found interesting, so I gave them a call and scheduled an assessment for her.

Karen was not very enthusiastic about the assessment, but she was very cooperative with the staff. I learned that Karen had allergies and food sensitivities. I was overwhelmed with all the information I received. I left with a lot to think about and many lifestyle changes to consider.

The assessment confirmed some of the things I already knew; red dyes pull zinc out of the body and too much sugar can weaken the immune system by as much as 50%, as well as decrease brain function. I wondered if Karen might have an allergy to chlorine, because she spends a lot of time swimming in the summer and would have to blow her nose excessively. When I asked her medical doctor about it, he just shrugged it off and ignored the question. Her whole child assessment revealed a concern that Karen did have an allergy to chlorine.

By adjusting her diet, we found that Karen was moodier and harder to reason with when she had too much sugar. When she is having a bad day, we can usually trace it to what she has eaten. She still has good and bad days, but the bad days are fewer.

She loves school and works hard. Her current teacher feels Karen is doing great on her daily work and is not concerned that she doesn't test well. I have learned that if her teacher breaks up the test into smaller parts and puts Karen in a room with fewer distractions, she performs better.

Through the Whole Child Institute, I feel I have learned there are things I can do to maintain some control over various aspects of my daughter's life. I have learned different ways to be an advocate in the school system for Karen, so she gets the attention she needs. To manage her behavior, she and I have worked on negotiating. The dietary changes we've made improve her general health and allow her to have a more positive attitude toward others. As a parent, it has been rewarding to see the changes in Karen emerge as I continue to implement what I've learned."

Karen's self-confidence is soaring these days. Through Kumon Math and Reading she has learned to compete against herself. Karen has been faithfully helping her gymnastics team to qualify for further competition. She has placed first on floor and beam and second for all-around competition. She will soon be traveling to Las Vegas, Nevada for more competition. Go, Karen!!

Chapter Eighteen

Ben came for a whole child assessment after his father began a search for alternative treatments for Ben's ADD. During the assessment, we noticed it was difficult for him to focus on just one thing. He had a tough time standing in a room without gravitating toward a wall or a table. Leaning on things seemed to help him to know where his body was in space. His speech was slurred and garbled. We believe that Ben's early medical history as well as poor nutrition led to his ADD. Ritalin only caused his already weakened immune system to become worse. His mother was doubtful that he could get anything out of the Kumon Math program because he had so many problems focusing on his work. Here is her story:

"Ben was born with hypertonia which is a muscular type of syndrome. He had delays in speech, walking and fine motor skills. When he was a baby, toddler and preschooler, he had many ear infections and was on antibiotics quite frequently. He also had pneumonia a couple of times; once he was even hospitalized for five days. We had him in daycare and doctors told us that if we wanted a healthy child, we should take him out. We did that, but he remained a sickly child.

Before he reached age three we enrolled him in speech therapy because he did not have a very large vocabulary. He also went to an Early Childhood Special Education (ECSE) class. When he started morning kindergarten, he then went to ECSE for the rest of the day. By the end of kindergarten, his speech was at an age appropriate level and thus he did not qualify for Special Education even though his fine motor skills were still lagging and the ECSE staff said they were still concerned. They also said there was nothing in the school system to address that problem. What they were really saying was that the school system did not want to spend the money and their hands were tied by the 'powers that be.'

Through first and second grade, Ben seemed to do okay with his schoolwork. He also started to show that he could read, but his comprehension was not progressing to where it should be. As third grade approached his speech became a problem once again. His third grade teacher alerted us to Ben's short attention span and suggested we visit our family doctor to see if he had ADD and needed Ritalin.

Our pediatrician put Ben on a three-week regimen to try the drug. One week he took a placebo, another week a certain dosage of Ritalin, and another week a heavier dosage, not necessarily in that order. Only the doctor knew what dosage Ben was getting. Based upon those three weeks, our doctor determined that Ritalin would help Ben and that he did have ADD. The teacher told us that when he was on Ritalin, she could really see a difference.

Ben had been on Ritalin for about six months when we became concerned about some of the side effects he was experiencing. He wasn't sleeping, and he had no appetite. As an underweight child he couldn't afford to lose any weight. His father went to a class discussion about ADD and healthy alternatives to Ritalin. He was looking for any answer outside of Ritalin because of the way Ben was reacting to it. At the class they had brochures for the Whole Child Institute.

The following day we scheduled Ben for a whole child assessment. Even though Ben had a hard time sitting, paying attention, and knowing where he was in space, he was pretty interested in the whole thing. Based on the resources the Whole Child Institute led us to, we changed his diet somewhat. We discontinued white breads and yellow cheeses and we cut down on sugar. We stopped using Ritalin. With the help of a clinical nutritionist, we put him on some natural food supplements, a multi-vitamin, a multi-mineral, Lethicin, B-complex, and Zinc Picolinate. At home we liked the way he was without the Ritalin much better. At school, the teachers still felt that maybe his attention problems would be helped by using it.

We also saw a psychologist during the summer before he started fifth grade. Based on her testing he was a low-to-average functioning child. She told us, 'Don't expect much from him. He might be brain damaged. He's not very intelligent. School will always be a struggle for him.' We felt that she was trying to label him as a slow learner with no hope.

We have been pressured by the school to have testing done by a neurologist. Right now Ben is participating in speech therapy. The teachers still feel that his, attentional, difficulties would be helped by Ritalin. They are not expressing that verbally, but we sense they want us to put him back on the drug. It is sad they don't become more educated themselves and realize there is life beyond Ritalin. We are still committed to discovering why Ben is dealing with symptoms of ADD and changing things for him at a cause and core level.

We have always been open to any drug-free changes we could make. The staff at the Whole Child Institute had a lot of good points, as far as seeking the least invasive treatments which would alleviate, rather than mask his symptoms. We liked their idea of teaching him proper posture while doing academics. We were impressed, and wanted to learn more about how to help Ben deal with his problems based on their experience and ideas.

I had a hard time believing Ben could function independently and stay on task at the Kumon Center, but Ben became an independent learner within his first three months of Kumon. He studied everyday and visited the center twice a week. He continued to need to be told to stay on task from time to time.

The whole child assessment made us aware of the nutritional part of Ben's problems. We learned how food could be affecting him and how sugar played a part in his patterns. My husband was open to this because of books and articles that he had read when he was researching this on his own. I was skeptical that Ben could make as many changes as he actually has.

Whole Child Institute

The educational specialist at the Whole Child Institute recommended that we go through the Kumon Math program and I think that has helped Ben to get organized and to stay on task. I feel it has been good for his self-confidence too. He began Kumon learning to trace lines. Now, he can divide faster than the average adult and is currently working on fractions. He is also beginning to enjoy the Kumon Reading program.

A major challenge for Ben to date is his reading comprehension. He also struggles to stay current with his homework. His dad works with him making sure it gets done, and also makes sure he understands what he is doing. He is learning quite a bit. As we compare this years grades to last year's, he has moved up from the lower groups in every subject. He is really doing well!

The teacher who works with him in the classroom has also spent time with the educational specialist from the Whole Child Institute and the two of them have come up with a way to work with Ben. We have discovered that when it comes to taking tests, he just wants to rush through them and finish everything as soon as he can. So his teacher has been giving him his tests in smaller increments. His teacher cuts his test papers in strips and gives Ben four problems at a time. He's been coming home with E's (Excellent) on math tests and other subjects. It's encouraging to see that.

Recently, Ben took a national standardized test at school and scored very, very low, but in no way did it reflect how he is really doing in the classroom. In other words, he still doesn't test well. The learning specialist at the Whole Child Institute feels that he would have realistic test scores if the test was given in separate subjects and someone sat with him while he was being tested. I couldn't agree more.

Initially, Ben was having a major problem with organization. His desk was always messy. His teacher and the WCI Educational Specialist came up with an idea to try to help him keep his things straight and orderly so he can easily transition from subject to subject. Ben also tends to want to interrupt the teacher when he has something on his mind, and doesn't wait to express it. He needs to learn when to speak and when not to, especially in school. The teacher is working hard on that and Ben is picking it up. I think it's an issue that is important for him to overcome. He can understand that interruptions and outbursts are socially inappropriate and that he needs to exercise self-control. He is continually improving in this area.

My present challenge is to help Ben be able to get comfortable in middle school next year because it will be a new environment for him. His teacher and other staff members at the elementary school are working with the middle school staff. There will be a time when we will all sit together and discuss how to help him. We may have someone in the school with him to make sure that he is doing what he is supposed to be doing and that he is organized. If he needs help, this person will be there to help him. The teachers will give him his tests in smaller pieces and continue doing the things that seem to be working with him this year.

We are very careful about what Ben takes into his system these days. One day at the Kumon Center, his instructor noticed that he was slurring his speech. He hadn't had anything unusual to eat that day, but I found out later that while at school he was given an over-the-counter antihistamine. Earlier in the year I had signed a form stating what kinds of over-the-counter medications could be given to Ben at school. After learning that the antihistamine probably would have an adverse affect on him, I forgot to change his emergency form at school, so of course, they gave it to him.

His health has really improved through this whole process. He looks better physcially. He's acting more responsible. His grades are higher. The challenge is to keep going. He still has a ways to go and I think he can improve more. The challenge for us as parents, is to keep working with him to do that. My husband and I have enjoyed a very positive working relationship with the Whole Child Institute, and we have been very happy with the changes we are seeing in our son."

Ben looks like a whole new child these days. He is walking taller, smiling more, and is able to engage in good eye contact appropriately. He no longer needs someone next to him in order to help him stay on task while doing his Kumon. In fact, as his mother stated earlier, he became an independent learner within his first few months at the Kumon Center. His maturational age has taken quite a leap and his improved math and reading comprehension abilities continue to astound those who are involved in his life.

Chapter Nineteen

"If you want to help children, you have to start looking at the brain; after all, they don't read with their kidneys."

—Jane M. Healy from *Endangered Minds*

Introduction To Balance—All body parts must work together in order to create a balanced, well-developed body and personality. As the above quote notes, a healthy brain is especially important. Our brain is a computer that runs on electricity. It is a network of tiny microscopic nerves, which go into the body from the spinal column, innervating every part of the body. The brain has storehouses of electricity located in the frontal portions of the cerebrum and back portions of the cerebellum. The cerebrum is responsible for memory, thinking and expression. The cerebellum is constantly on guard making sure the brain maintains its optimum electrical capacity. The brain coordinates all the muscles and their various functions, keeping us alert during undue stress and fatigue.

Many structures and fluids in the skull must work together for correct brain function. The brain floats in a pool of saltwater. It is protected by the mastoid glands, which provide the brain with antibodies and nutrition. The ears control the balance of the body by generating electricity that flows out of the ears and picks up sounds in the environment. The orbits of the eyes pick up light energy that is used to see. They also furnish the frontal lobes of the brain with energy in order to provide the body with balance. The openings of the nostrils drain excess brain and sinus fluid from the head and vent oxygen to and from the ventricles of the brain. The pituitary gland, housed below the brain, controls the release of hormones. These hormones are especially vital to newborns for developing the brain, personality, and sexuality. Hormones, primarily produced and released by the thyroid and the adrenal glands, create most of the electricity for the brain. Electricity is also produced by electrolyte minerals—in the blood and lymphatic system, glycogen made by the liver, and external electricity from the environment picked up by hairs on the head. A specific hormone, Dopamine, is a neurotransmitter, which is secreted and stored in nerve endings. When Dopamine combines with protein, it changes the permeability of a cell. Therefore, Dopamine levels have a great deal to do with how the body assimilates nutrition and expels antioxidants on the cellular level. When there is an imbalance in any part of the nervous system or its back-up systems, the body, mind and/or personality begin to deteriorate. Balanced body chemistry is crucial in order to lead a happy, healthy life. Rewritten by Linda Vettrus with permission from Dawn (Versendaal) Hoezee, author of *Contact Reflex Analysis and Designed Clinical Nutrition A Healing Art.*

Water—In the body, there is a balance to be maintained between the electricity and the fluid in the body. It is said that the human body is composed of 75% water and 25% solid mass. Brain tissue is composed of 85% water. Just as the cardiovascular and respiratory systems have a rhythm to maintain, there exists an equally important "hydraulic" system that needs to be maintained for the whole body, especially the brain. Dr. Batmanghelidj, author of *Your Body's Many Cries For Water*, states, "...dehydration causes stress and stress will cause further dehydration." Keeping the body hydrated reduces stress.

Electrical Flow—Sensitivity to electromagnetic forces is a potential factor in behavioral problems. Electricians know that electrical energy flows easier into the left hand of the body and exits through the right hand. If an electrician is unsure about the presence of a "live" wire, he will be sure to handle a circuit or outlet with his right hand avoiding major shock. At the Whole Child Institute we have noticed that several children who wore their watch on their right wrist and changed to wearing their watch on their left wrist, experienced improved behavior. Perhaps by wearing the watch on the right wrist created a back up of negative energy. Those affected by electro-magnetic stress from the battery in a watch became even more balanced when not wearing the watch at all.

Body/Brain Connection—To the experienced observer, it is easy to recognize that in so many children who have learning disabilities and/or behavior challenges, the brain is not in control of the body. When a child cannot do fairly simple movements and coordinated activities such as the Cross Crawls from Brain Gym™, (touching right hand to raised left knee and vice versa) there is a body-brain connection difficulty. Research has shown that certain movements, especially those involving crossing the mid-line of the body have a direct influence upon the functioning of the brain and have a very calming, therapeutic effect. After one performs these exercises, the brain is truly able to be in command of the body and there is an obvious balance in the body/brain connection. Therefore, by improving body/brain connections, emotional behavior becomes calmer and more balanced. Emotions are inseparable from thought and must be properly controlled in order to achieve improved health and well-being.

Chronological Age vs. Maturational Age—When children are dealing with developmental delays there can be a considerable difference between chronological age (actual years old) and maturational age. A general formula for computing the maturational age for some children dealing with ADHD (Attention Deficit Hyperactivity Disorder) is to subtract one-third of their chronological age. For example: Age 12 minus 4 equals age 8. (4 being one-third of 12). So, a child dealing with ADHD who is twelve years old chronologically, might maturationally be eight years old. Adults that deal with these children, will often comment, "Grow up!" Kids labeled with ADD/ADHD often need extra time to mature. They feel more comfortable with younger children than with their peers, and seem to be very good at relating to their needs. Reversely some children, that we have seen through whole child assessments, are maturationally 'adults' trapped inside children's bodies. These children have difficulty with parental authority since they are already thinking like adults, yet legally and otherwise, they must endure the role of being a minor. A considerable discrepancy in maturational and chronological age, one way or the other, tends to create a great deal of stress.

Intelligences

Seven Intelligences—Professor Howard Gardner of Harvard University developed the Theory of the Seven Intelligences. This theory is fully outlined in his book, *Frames of Mind* which was expanded for school use in *The Unschooled Mind.* The Seven Intelligences are defined in the following list.

> *Linguistic Intelligence*—is the ability to read, write and communicate with words. This skill is highly developed in authors, poets, and orators.

> *Logical Intelligence*—is better known as mathematical intelligence. It is the ability to reason and calculate. This intelligence is highly developed in scientists, lawyers mathematicians, and judges.

Traditionally, IQ tests have focused on linguistic intelligence and logical intelligence. Gardner says, "...this has given us a warped and limited view of our learning potential." He lists five more distinct intelligences.

> *Musical Intelligence*—is highly developed in composers, conductors and top musicians.

Spatial or Visual Intelligence—is used by architects, sculptors, painters, navigators, and pilots. Some believe that these are two separate but closely related functions.

Kinesthetic Intelligence or Physical Intelligence—is highly developed in athletes, dancers, gymnasts and perhaps surgeons.

Interpersonal Intelligence—is the ability to relate to others. This is the kind of ability that seems natural with salesmen, motivators, and negotiators.

Intrapersonal or Introspective Intelligence—is the ability of insight, to know oneself. It is the kind of ability that allows one to tap into the tremendous bank of information stored in the subconscious mind.

Stroke patients, brain surgery, and research have helped us to see that these intelligences are real. Severe damage to a certain area of the brain housing one of these "intelligences" or abilities supports Dr. Gardner's theory. In their book, *The Learning Revolution,* authors Gordon Dryden and Jeannette Vos, Ed.D. note that others believe that "spacial" and "visual" intelligence are two separate but closely related functions, thus giving us eight intelligences to consider.

IQ—Intelligence Quotient
IQ = <u>mental age</u> (age score received from an intelligence test)
<u>chronological age</u> (actual age since birth)
<u>divided</u> and <u>multiplied by 100</u>.

I.Q.—Intelligence Quotient Scale
Under 80 =   Various Mental Handicaps
80-89   =   Slow Learner
90-110   =   Average Intelligence
110-119 =   Bright or High Average
120-129 =   Superior Intelligence
Over 130 =   Gifted
Over 160 =   Superiorly Gifted or Genius

Alfred W. Munzert, Ph.D., in his book, *Test Your IQ,* (Third Edition), reminds us that, "...the critical factor of intelligence is its development and use." He says, "There are many reasons why IQ, particularly the results of one test, may not indicate a true level of intelligence and potential capability." At the Whole Child Institute we understand that children's true abilities are not always reflected by their I.Q. score. This is especially true for children dealing with brain allergies and/or toxins in their brains.

EQ: Emotional Intelligence—At the Whole Child Institute we consider emotional intelligence as well as mental intelligence. According to Daniel Goleman, author of *Emotional Intelligence: Why it can matter more than IQ,* "Emotional intelligence is the ability to understand one's feelings and feel empathy for another, the ability to motivate oneself and delay gratification, the ability to supress regression and be compassionate, the ability to communicate appropriately, cooperate, focus one's attention and make wise decisions." Goleman shares brain research, which explains why calm children with appropriate emotions can learn rapidly and why those who are an emotional wreck constantly struggle with academics. He discusses the two structures most responsible for emotional quality, the hippocampus and the amygdala which are deep within the subcortical lymbic system. "The amygdala acts as a storehouse of emotional memory, and thus is of significance itself. Life without the amygdala is a life stripped of personal meaning." Without the amygdala there is no interest in human connections. No tears, no passion, no soothing comfort, no sense of despair or frustration. The hippocampus remembers the factual information while the amygdala remembers the emotional overtone. An experience is recorded together by these minute, yet powerful neighbors. Thus, the brain has two memory systems: One for ordinary facts and one for emotionally charged ones. Doctors report that patients with damage to the pre-frontal amygdala circuit show no decrease of

IQ, yet these people make very poor decisions. They have "lost access to their emotional learning" which is critical for rational decisions, thus, "the emotional brain is as involved in reasoning as is the thinking brain." (Comments by Launa Ellison, Consortium For Whole Brain Learning Volume 11, No. 2 Winter 1996.

Affirmations and Positive Self-Talk—Kids can get into a lot of negative self-talk when learning something that is challenging for them. The word "try" has been found to be a major "stressor." This word can be replaced with, "Do your best." It has been proven in teen competitions that these words have incredible results. Using positive affirmations in conversation or listening to Shad Helmstetter's Positive Self-Talk tapes can help balance emotional well-being. Dr. Helmstetter holds a Ph.D. in Motivational Psychology. His Positive Self-Talk tape series has helped many challenging children. In one series, *Self-Esteem for Older Kids*, a child might hear, "I am good at dealing with problems. I am good at dealing with any problem I face." or "You get along well with others, in fact, you make it a point to get along well." Parents may choose to play a positive affirmation or self-talk tape while their children are going to sleep at night. When creating your own self-talk tapes be sure to use the voice of an unfamiliar person. The content will be more believable to the listener if they do not recognize the voice. Some of the Whole Child Institute's favorite affirmations are as follows:

- I am even-tempered and fair-minded.
- I am capable of connecting and contributing.
- I am respectful.
- I am responsible.
- I am safe.
- I am prepared.
- When I hear the word "TRY," I do my "BEST."
- I am lovable and capable.

Thinkers/Feelers—In order to attain balance within a family, one needs to consider the basic internal traits and personalities of each family member. Thinkers and feelers deal with situations and relationships differently. "Some of us lead with our heads and others with our hearts," says Mary Sheedy Kurchinka, author of *Raising Your Spirited Child.* Thinkers tend to look at the facts. Feelers, on the other hand, respond to what happens and the emotional impact that it has on them. Feelers have to overcome their hurt before tackling the source of their pain. In an article in Parents' Magazine, Mary Sheedy Kurcinka writes, "Although all children consider both their thoughts and feelings in their daily lives, over time a basic preference for one or the other emerges. The preference is far less a choice than the result of the child's inborn temperament. Each trait is unique and one is not superior to the other. What is crucial is the way a parent, teacher or caregiver responds to a child based on his or her particular bent."

Thinkers

- Value personal achievement.
- Become easily upset if unable to learn quickly.
- Some perform poorly in school.
- Need opportunities to show their competence.
- Tend to have enjoyed doing things by themselves since they were toddlers.
- Need justice, fairness, and answers.
- Have a constant need to know why things have to be done in a particular way.
- Place a high value on truth.
- Any type of unfairness upsets them and they insist that everyone, plays by the rules no matter what the outcome.
- Prefer detailed feedback; general praise is regarded with suspicion.
- Prefer to solve a problem before considering feelings.

Feelers

- Need a hug before dealing with an issue.
- Need to vent emotions before addressing a problem.
- Need help learning to use words for their feelings rather than hitting or screaming.
- Need encouragement to stand up for things that are important to them.
- Concerned with making sure no one is left out.

Learning Styles—Dr. Anthony I. Gregore's research concerning learning styles provides invaluable insights. Cynthia Ulrich Tobias agrees and addresses learning style diferences very effectively in her two books, *The Way They Learn* and *Every Child Can Learn.* She states in her book, *The Way They Learn*, that Dr. Gregore's research is "...one of the most effective models for understanding learning style differences." She includes excellent charts outlining Gregore's findings. She concludes that section by saying, "Just because your children aren't responding to you, doesn't mean they aren't listening. It could be that the difference in your perspective is so great that you sometimes might as well be living in different countries and speaking different languages." Just as some cannot "carry a tune," some do not learn well visually! These in-abilities have nothing to do with a child's potential or their innate ability to learn. Learning styles are neurologically based. People are born with strengths and weaknesses in their learning patterns.

Learning Byte—According to Dr. Lyelle Palmer, head of Special Education at Winona State University in Winona Minnesota, the human byte is between two and seven with the average byte being four or five. Learning byte means how much information, in a particular category, a person can hold for a twenty-four hour period. If for example a child has a byte of three, for spelling, and is taught four spelling words, twenty-four hours latter he will not have just forgotten the extra word that went over his byte. The extra word will have blown all of his fuses and twenty-four hours later he will have forgotten all four spelling words.

Patterned Learners—Visual learners learn from what they see, auditory learners learn from what they hear, and hands-on learners or kinesthetic learners learn by using their hands while incorporating other senses. Patterned Learners learn by having information taught directly into their mid-brain according to their learning byte. Linda Vettrus, Director of the Whole Child Institute, discovered this very important learning style. The following are excerpts from her new book, *Johnny Can Read and Do Math.* "Everyone can benefit from the teaching methods that work for this particular learning style. It is a known fact that the Whole Language theory only works with about 80% of students, leaving 20% of the student body floundering. Concerned about this minority of students and her own need to be taught in a way she learns best, Linda began to recognize many similarities. These learners need concrete information given to them. They learn best by being taught an answer and then being asked the question. For example, teaching the color red would sound like this: 'This color is red. What color is it?' If the student was first asked, 'What color is this?' and then had to guess the answer, the student might guess four different colors. There after, as a patterned learner, he would then have to shuffle through all the incorrect responses, unsure which response was correct. Even if he knew the correct response he would still need to shuffle through the incorrect information he had patterned when learning about the color red. Every time he would be presented with the color red, he would have to shuffle through four different responses. A patterned learner will pattern mistakes onto his brain and have a difficult time unlearning them. Children who process slowly, tend to be labeled ADD, Autisic, Slow Learner, or Learning Disabled. Many of these children are mislabeled and are actually patterned learners. Also children who have these challenges tend to be patterned learners. All learners benefit from patterned learning. However, for those children who are Patterned Learners it is the only way they are truly successful. The Learning Gap Therapy Program, developed at the Whole Child Institute, works especially well for patterned learners. Once new information has been learned, Maria Montessori's Three Period Lesson can be effective. For severe patterned learners, Kumon Math and Reading may be the only way they can learn.

Patterned Learners

- Need limited instructional words.
- Teachable when hearing and repeating one word at a time, staying within their learning byte.
- Usually need physical activity when learning.
- Learn best by hearing the answer first, then the question.
- Pattern mistakes onto their brain easily, but have a difficult time getting these mistakes out of their brain. Will keep responding with the wrong answers or will sift through incorrect responses.
- Need to learn things in order and only when they have mastered the order should they practice "out of order."

Spatial Difficulties

- Difficulty knowing where one is in space, may need to lean on tables,etc.
- Difficulty sorting puzzle pieces into piles: corner, top, bottom, side, inside.
- Difficulty with body/brain connection activities.

Maria Montessori's Three Period Lesson—This lesson is used to reinforce what has been patterned. The first period consists of identifying the object. "This block is red. This one is yellow. This one is blue." The items are mixed up and identified several times. In the second period the learner listens and plays various recognition games like following directions— point to the yellow one, hide the red one, and so on. The third period is the test phase of learning when the learner correctly answers the question, "What color is this block?" This method is great for young learners, but is also effective for those struggling at higher grade levels and can be modified to fit their level of learning.

Maria Montessori's Practical Life/Absorbent Mind— Learning the value of work early on is important for adding balance and success to a child's life. Children need to become comfortable with the word "work" and internalize it as a wonderful part of their lives. Maria Montessori taught that "work" for a child is purposeful activity that is necessary for developing self-esteem, positive attitudes, concentration and independence. Activities such as folding a washcloth, sweeping up crumbs, washing a tabletop, and properly lifting and carrying a chair, are tasks that can be done even by preschoolers. Parents should encourage children to do whatever they are capable of doing. This means that when a child has learned to walk, he should not be carried except when expedience is necessary. When children are capable of cleaning up spilled milk, let them do it. Natural consequences are great teachers. Encouraging helpfulness with a positive attitude will help children become service-oriented leaders of tomorrow.

Brain Gym™—The Brain Gym™ Program revolves around simple and enjoyable activities, many of which involve crossing the midline of the body. These exercises empower students of any age by drawing out potentials locked inside their own bodies. Paul Dennison, creator of Brain Gym™ states, "...some children try too hard and switch off the brain integration mechanism necessary for complete learning." He feels that, "The solution is whole brain learning through movement re-patterning and Brain Gym™ activities. These activities enable students to access those parts of the brain previously unavailable to them. The changes in learning and behavior are often immediate and profound. Children discover how to receive information and express themselves simultaneously."

Carla Hannaford, Ph.D., in her book, *Smart Moves—Why learning is not all in your head*, states, "I am greatly indebted to Paul Dennison who, in his struggle to find a way through his own dyslexia and visual difficulties put together the Brain Gym™ program." Research projects using Brain Gym™ have sprung up all over the world since Dr. Dennison opened the Educational Kinesiology Foundation in 1987. Dr. Hannaford states, "...simple, natural, drug-free tools like Brain Gym™ can assist us as we consciously undertake to eliminate all the...labels, concealing the intelligent learner underneath." Our resource guide contains information for contacting a Brain Gym™ Instructor.

Dyslexia: Davis Perceptual Ability Assessment and Davis Orientation Counseling—Ronald Davis, although gifted, talented, creative, and imaginative was labeled "retarded" by his schoolteachers. He grew up wondering why he couldn't learn in school. After becoming aware of his own dyslexia as an adult, he made the startling discovery that dyslexia is actually a unique learning style. He has written about his discovery in his book, *The Gift of Dyslexia*. This book takes the reader beyond understanding and offers a practical screening process and solutions for the truly dyslexic. Ron walks the reader through his Perceptual Ability Assessment and thoroughly explains his therapy called Davis Orientation Counseling. The entire book helps anyone understand that dyslexia is truly a gift. The gift is used when those dealing with dyslexia use disorientation on an unconscious level in order to see multi-dimensionally and can perceive things from more than one perspective. When a person is gifted with dyslexia and begins to use language, there is potential for developing a learning disability. Disorientation becomes a problem when a child is reading. Many parents of children who are challenged by learning can relate to the description of disorientation, while reading Ron's book.

Learning Gap Therapy—Linda Vettrus, co-founder of the Whole Child Institute and co-author of this book, developed the

Whole Child Institute

Whole Child Institute's Learning Gap Therapy Program which connects the body and brain bringing performance up to a student's intelligence level. This therapy slows down the brain and places information into the mid-brain (automatic brain) at 100% accuracy, while staying within a student's learning byte. Some of this educational therapy can be found in her book, *Johnny Can Read and Do Math*, available through the Whole Child Institute. A students learning byte is the amount of information a student is able to retain within a twenty-four hour period. Her Learning Gap Therapy is based on an adaptation to the Writing Road to Reading curriculum, a forty year old program developed by Romalda Spalding. Dr. Samuel T. Orton of the Orton Dyslexia society developed the phonograms or letter chunks for this program. The prepatory adaptation requires a student to focus attention on their fingers which are connected at the mid-line of their body. A unique pencil grasp is used during this therapy in order to shut down the front area of the brain and allow information to flow freely from mid-brain to the writing hand and back. The front area of the brain is the part of the brain that does not work well for those dealing with ADD/ADHD, because the neurotransmitters have a difficult time connecting in that area of the brain. This therapy bypasses the front area of the brain and brings information into mid-brain at 100% accuracy. A word is given by the therapist and repeated by the student until the entire sentence of instruction is stated. The student then performs the instruction given. In this particular therapy, the listening, processing and regurgitation of information comes before a precise programmed movement. Students' visual, auditory, and sensory integration processing improves with this therapy. For some patterned learners as in Kumon math and reading, it may be the only way they can learn. This therapy supplements Kumon reading and can be easily learned by parents and thus is very cost effective. Contact the Whole Child Institute for information on ordering this program.

Puzzles—Jigsaw puzzles can be a great quiet time activity. Children can develop interpersonal skills while putting a puzzle together with others. Puzzles can help develop sequential thinking and good visual/spatial skills. Sorting the pieces into stacks of corner pieces, top pieces, bottom pieces, side pieces, and inside pieces, then strategically placing these pieces in their appropriate locations, (first, corner pieces in the corners, then, top edge pieces at the top, next, side edge pieces at the sides, bottom edge pieces at the bottom, and then, placing the inside pieces in the center) is a great way to teach a child organizational and spacial skills. There are many benefits to be gained from puzzles, board games, and construction toys found in a "quality" childrens' toy store. Educational Consultants from Discovery Toys are always available to explain how toys can fit into the various stages of child development. Contact Discovery Toys for a consultant in your neighborhood.

Discovery Toys—Discovery Toy's founder, female entrepenuer, Lane Nemeth, believes that play is the work of the child and toys are their tools. She has dedicated her life to developing a company that helps parents and caregivers understand the importance of developmental stages and the learning that needs to go on during those stages. Besides playing with Discovery Toys, we at the Whole Child Institute believe that children also benefit greatly if they are encouraged to be young entrepreneurs. Having a desire for a big item, like a bike or portable stereo can be a great motivator for a child to earn money. This situation also presents a young person with a problem that needs to be solved. Enterprising, ambitious young people manage to earn money when the willingness to work and serve is balanced with the desire to obtain something. Flyers can be created and distributed to senior citizens and young mothers, for example, letting them know of the youth's availability to mow a lawn, wash a car, rake leaves, or babysit. The list is endless for young people who have acquired the skills and maturity needed to offer services to others.

Problems encountered with children who come to the Whole Child Institute and therapies that may be used to overcome some of their challenges.

Stress—Wayne Topping, in his book *Success Over Stress*, explains the difference between positive and negative stress. He refers to positive stress as *"eustress."* He writes, "With eustress, we feel stimulated, productive, energetic, optimistic, and in control as we deal with a challenging event." On the other hand negative stress can lead to feelings of helplessness, frustration, and disappointment and can be responsible for depression, headaches, stomach aches and a host of other physical conditions. Learning and applying stress reduction techniques is the key to attaining a balance between positive and negative stress. Adults can model these techniques for children, teaching them by example how to overcome the negative effects of stress.

Adolescent Depression—Lili Frank Garfinkel, of PACER: Juvenile Justice Project makes several excellent points in her article *Adolescent Depression: A Slide into Chaos*, published in The PACESETTER in February of 1995. Depression comes in many "disguises." Danger signs of depression are not dramatic and are easily missed. Warning signs of depression are…

- Persistent feelings of worthlessness, failure, and/or extreme sadness.
- Inability to believe one is really loved.
- Persistent dramatic mood swings.
- Changes in appetite.
- Blaming others when things go wrong.
- Disturbances in sleep patterns.
- Persistent feelings of fatigue or vague illness (headaches, stomach aches).
- Trouble concentrating on work (often mistaken for ADD/ADHD).

- Morbid thoughts—preoccupation with illness, death, and funerals.
- Body language usually reads "Go away, I hate you!"

Here are some resources she suggests to parents for finding help for a depressed child. The books, *No One Saw My Pain*, co-written by Dr. Andrew Slaby and Lili Frank Garfinkel and *A Guidebook For Parents of Children with EBD,* both books are available from PACER Center (Parent Advocacy Center Educational Resource Center) 4826 Chicago Ave. So., Minneapolis, MN 55417-1098, (612) 827-2966, website: http://www.pacer.org. Also, national and state organizations offer hotlines. Doctors and psychiatrists can tell you the symptoms of depression. Doctors of preventive medicine know a great deal about the physical cause and core of depression.

Asthma—Asthma steals breath from children and ranks as one of the nation's worse health epidemics. According to the American Lung Association, Asthma is a life-threatening chronic inflammation of the upper airways that affects twelve million people nationwide. The incidence of asthma has doubled since 1980. Studies show that new construction practices may contribute to the rise in this disease. Sick building syndrome is created by tighter construction techniques, inadequate ventilation, and toxic building materials. In the chapter Our Toxic World, our readers can get a clearer picture of why asthma is on the rise. Our chapter entitled, Early Intervention, is a great story about a little boy named Keith who has since overcome his struggle with asthma. This story shows how sometimes an already suppressed system can be worsened by the use of medication. Finding the cause and core and treating childhood asthma at that level may be the best treatment in some cases.

Diabetes/Hypoglycemia—About two years ago a popular medical journal, *The Lancet,* came out with a statement relating diabetes to a dairy allergy. It went something like this: The number one leading cause of diabetes in children is a dairy allergy. Hypoglycemia, (blood sugar imbalance) is often under diagnosed and hence, not addressed as a health issue. This imbalance in the body then leads to Candida (yeast) over growth. When Candida grows out of control, one may become sick with Chronic Fatigue Syndrome and eventually the Epstein-Barr Virus and possibly other chronic illnesses like diabetes. By recognizing signs of hypoglycemia and taking appropriate action early on, chronic illness can often be avoided.

As we look at the body clinically and nutritionally, ADD can be seen in some children as a blood sugar imbalance. ADHD is caused, in this point of view, when that imbalance is so "out of whack" the adrenal glands are overproducing causing hormonal changes, which can lead to anger and rage. Schools refer to students at that stage as having EBD (Emotional Behavior Disorder).

Colon Health—Diabetes, thyroid deficiency, constipation, fatigue, poor eyesight, hearing loss, asthma, colds, allergies, digestive problems; gas, abdominal pain, and more, are according to Dr. Norman W. Walker, afflictions which stem from an unhealthy colon, or large intestine. In the book, *Colon Health*, author Dr. Norman W. Walker states, "The elimination of undigested food and other waste products is equally as important as the proper digestion and assimilation of food. Few of us realize that failure to effectively eliminate waste products from the body causes so much fermentation and putrification in the large intestine or colon, that the neglected accumulation of such waste can, and frequently does result in a lingering demise." When waste material in the body are not properly disposed of, toxemia and toxic poisons are the end result. At that point, the body begins to show physical signs like those mentioned in the beginning of this section.

Colon irrigation, known as colonics, are obtainable from certified colon therapists. By looking under colonics or colon irrigations in the yellow pages, one may find people trained in this area. Naturopaths, chiropractors and physiotherapists may also have colonic equipment and training in that area. When the colon is coated with fecal incrustation it is unable to work effectively and becomes, according to Dr. Walker, "....a generator of toxicity to the detriment of health, happiness, and longevity." Toxemia results from the lining of the colon being blocked. Any nutritional elements end up going into the bloodstream as polluted products. Toxemia, according to Dr. Walker, "...is a condition in which the blood contains poisonous products which are produced by the growth of pathogenic or disease-producing bacteria. Pimples, for example are usually the first sign that toxemia has found its way into the body." Dr. Walker's book, *Colon Health: The Key to a Vibrant Life!* is a must read for anyone wanting to have a better understanding of their health. We also recommend Dr. William Crook's book, *Help For The Hyperactive Child*, where you can find pictures that show the simple end results of imbalance within the intestines, known as Candida Albicans.

Chiropractic—Chiropractic care offers help to children with learning, behavioral, emotional, and neurological problems. Chiropractic is a misunderstood medical specialty. Doctors of chiropractic are the only members of the healthcare profession who have specialized training in recognizing and analyzing body imbalances, muscle tensions and spinal misalignments.

The nervous system is the center for learning, memory, thought, and consciousness, allowing connections to be made between one's inner and outer world. All internal organs receive a nerve supply from the spine. Pilot studies have confirmed clinical findings that chiropractic care has a positive effect on anxiety, inability to concentrate, low mental stamina, hyperactivity, discipline problems, low grades, and even IQ scores. Researchers have noted success with Dyslexia, Learning Disabilities, and Attention Deficit Disorder. Chiropractic holds the promise of a non-chemical way of caring for challenging children. For instance, if a doctor determines that ankle adjustments are needed, it is essential that a child have them done. The ankles protect the large nerve meridians that circulate a generous amount of electrical energy throughout the body. This electrical energy is needed for brain power, memory, eyesight, hearing, pancreas function and constant/perfect balance and posture. Many of the children seen at the Whole Child Institute have shown a need for Chiropractic care.

Contact Reflex Analysis(sm) (CRAsm)—The nervous system is the center for learning, memory, thought, and consciousness, which connects one's inner and outer world. Contact Reflex Analysis(sm) is a simple, safe, natural method of analyzing the body's structural, physical, and nutritional needs. It is a means by which doctors use the body's reflexes to accurately determine the root cause of a health problem and like other types of Kinesiology (muscle testing), is not a method of diagnosis. Dr. D. A.Versendaal, the researcher and developer of CRA(sm) believes that it helps a practitioner to find health problems before they become full-blown. Dr. Versendaal worked with a medical doctor, a clinical nutritionist, and a hemotologist for thirty years while developing CRA(sm). He is confident that CRA(sm)
quickly and accurately uncovers the root of a health problem and provides a doctor with answers for correcting it. CRA(sm) has been taught in continuing education seminars across the United States to all types of health professionals for over twenty-five years. **Contact Reflex Analysis and CRA are service marks of Dawn (Versendaal) Hoezee, daughter of Dr. D.A. Versendaal.**

Homeopathy

"Homeopathy...cures a larger percentage of cases than any other method of treatment and is beyond all doubt, safer, more economical, and the most complete medical science."

—Mahatma Gandhi

Homeopathic remedies, from all realms of nature, gently stimulate the body to heal itself and are based on the idea that "like cures like." For instance if one is stung by a bee, the homeopathic remedy would be prepared by adding a minute amount of bee-sting venom to water thus creating the same electrical frequency found in a potent bee sting. Homeopathic remedies are aimed at correcting sensory network interference. Combining homeopathic formulas with regular chiropractic adjustments can help to build a healthy nervous system bringing sensitivity and life to the body. At the Whole Child Institute we agree with Yehude Menuhin who said, "Homeopathy is one of the rare medical approaches which carries no penalties, only benefits."

Psychotherapy—The goal of psychotherapy is to facilitate a person's understanding of an anxiety-causing life-problem in the hope that this understanding will bring about a positive change in behavior. Behavior modification techniques are used to bring about a more effective adjustment to an environment or situation. In psychotherapy a person gains insight into the cause and core of the problem. Behavior modification reinforces acceptable behaviors with rewards, but is considered very shallow in comparison to the resolution gained in psychotherapy. Never the less, behavior modification techniques are useful in managing "damage control" while digging deeper towards the real problem. Behavior modification reinforces positive behavior on a daily basis and is a reward based system. Psychotherapy helps a child explore new positive patterns of behavior.

A few tips in finding a psychotherapist to work with you...

- Find someone in private practice, who can give more freely to you without the constraints of an HMO.
- Find someone you feel good about being with that shares your beliefs, ideals, and values.

Whole Child Institute

- Find out whether they have the child's best interest at heart, a youth/child advocate, yet are supportive to your role as a parent.

CranioSacral Therapy—CranioSacral Massage is a non-invasive, gentle, manipulative therapy. The CranioSacral System is a physiological system that exists in humans and animals possessing a brain and spinal cord. An imbalance in the CranioSacral System can adversely affect the development and function of the brain and spinal cord, possibly resulting in sensory, motor and intellectual dysfunction. This therapy is being used by various health care professionals including osteopaths, medical doctors, doctors of chiropractic medicine, psychiatrists, psychologists, dentists, physical therapists, occupational therapists, accupuncturists, and licensed body workers.

At the Whole Child Institute, we have found that CranioSacral therapy is an effective way to balance the natural electrical flow of the body. We have witnessed children with Autism become more aware of their surroundings. Those dealing with ADD have been able to focus better. Children dealing with ADHD seem calmer and more balanced. We have also received reports of doctors lowering seizure medication for children who suffer from various types of seizure disorders.

Zone Therapy—This therapy has been proven successful in treating a variety of physical and emotional problems in children. Those dealing with Attention Deficit Disorder have experienced an increase in their concentration abilities and a decrease in their undesirable behavior. Parents of children with Autism have noted significant changes in behavior to the point where returning to a mainstream classroom has been possible. Parent's have also witnessed a quick reduction in allergy symptoms. Zone Therapy has enabled children with Down's Syndrome to become more proficient at walking and controlling their tongue. Children appear to intuitively know that the zone treatment is beneficial to them. One mother reported that her child cried when he was told she was unable to take him to one of his zone therapy appointments. Another benefit of Zone Therapy is that it brings balance to a child's body chemistry, resulting in children who start to crave healthier foods. Colds and flu symptoms can be alleviated if a child is treated during the first signs of onset.

For the Zone Therapist this therapy involves an in-depth understanding of how the body's healing systems can be activated by triggering points on the feet. The therapist uses deep pressure and strokes on various areas of the feet. Discomfort felt at specific points, communicates to the client and Zone Therapist where the body is out of balance and needing attention. By knowing how to activate individual trigger points, the therapist is able to send a message to the brain to clear the energy (electrical) blockage in the affected area of the body. In other words, the feet serve as the "keyboard" to the "computer", the brain, allowing the therapist to communicate with the client's body. This energy (electrical) balancing allows the body's own healing systems to "kick in" and correct specific problems. Zone Therapy is not always a quick fix, but a modality that allows the body to heal itself in regards to its own timeline.

Reflexology—Millions of people all around the world use a simple method called reflexology to positively affect the health and well-being of others. Reflexology is the study and practice of applying pressure to points on the hands and feet, which correspond to various parts of the body. Centers for brain-injured children in Scotland and the U.S. use reflexology as part of their sensory-motor exercises for rebuilding an injured nervous system.

Reflexology is a wonderful way for families to bond as well as relax together. Touch is a unique form of communication and establishes a strong link between child and adult. Childhood injuries, chronic conditions and growing pains can all be helped with reflexology. In the book, *A Parent's Guide to Reflexology: Helping your child overcome illness and injury through touch,* a book by Kevin and Barbara Kunz, includes a listing of conditions such as hyperactivity, learning difficulties, brain injuries, etc., as well as a list of technique applications for reflexology. This book is a wonderful introduction to the benefits and "how-tos" of reflexology such as:

- Preventing illness.
- Sharpening and strengthening a child's reflexes.
- Relaxation techniques for childhood stress.
- How to build a family reflexology wellness program.

Touch For Health—*Touch for Health—A practical guide to natural health, using accupressure, touch, and massage to improve postural balance and reduce physical and mental pain and tension* by John F. Thie, D.C. teaches Dr. Thie's approach for restoring our natural energies. This teaching gives the general public safe and easy techniques for attaining a healthy balance. As described in the Bible, all that's needed is a pair of loving hands for healing to take place, even though science does not understand why.

Health Kinesiology—Health Kinesiology is a synthesis of Touch for Health and other kinesiologies, which have come before it. Health Kinesiology is a comprehensive healing modality combining artful intuition with various sciences including physics, anatomy and physiology.

Science of Personology—Personology is a science that has been around for over fifty years, and yet no one seems to have heard about it. It is the study of human beings through their physical structure and is the synergistic culmination of years of research/analysis by many scientists and philosophers. It adds a new dimension to the understanding of human behavior. There is a blending of genetics, physiology, anatomy and neurology to create a personality "blueprint" or profile unique for each individual. Over seventy structures in our physical make-up have been correlated scientifically and statistically validated with trait patterns in behavior. The knowledge and insight gained by learning about individuals through personology helps ease disharmony in marriages, and all kinds of relationships whether it be personal or job related. Personology can help children better understand their intrapersonal and interpersonal relationships as well as helping parents guide children on their own unique path.

Television—T.V. has stolen much of our childrens' interest in real life and has decreased their self-expression. Television is anti-social, encourages a short attention span, allows no time for critical reaction, and interrupts family conversation. After such a long list of negatives, is there even one positive? Yes, television is a great way to become informed and is very entertaining. Educationally speaking though, television is a visual modality that does not allow a viewer to practice visualization. In the days of radio shows children had the opportunity to learn and practice visualization skills. Math, spelling and reading comprehension scores were much higher in the "good old" days. Good visualization skills are needed in mathematics for carry-overs, borrowing, etc. It's important in spelling in order to see phonograms and sound them out. In reading, visualization is essential for good reading comprehension.

"Whoever tells the stories, defines the culture," says David Walsh, Ph.D., President of the National Institute on Media and the Family. This group is committed to maximizing the benefits and minimizing the harm of media on children and families through research, education, and advocacy. The organization states that the amount of time school-aged children spend watching TV is fifty-six times greater than the amount of time spent interacting with their fathers, and eleven times greater than interacting with their mothers. American children spend more time watching television than any other activity of their working lives. The average American child will witness 200,000 acts of violence on TV before he or she graduates from high school. "All television is educational. The question is, What does it teach?" said Nicholas Johnson, former Federal Communications Commission Chairman. The National Institute on Media and the Family and the Whole Child Institute believe that informed parents make better choices.

Art Therapy—Wouldn't it be great if all children were to replace an hour of TV everyday with the repeated expression of an art form? Music, dance, drama, creative play, and drawing are all great alternatives. This creative expression of themselves wouldn't necessarily require "lessons" or "teaching." Creative expression could very well be nurtured by items available in a child's environment, along with encouragement by significant others. Self-discipline, self-expression, development of a special talent, interpersonal intelligence, a sense of joy and accomplishment are some of the benefits of time spent in creative expression. Children don't copy what they see, they draw the inner reality of what is important to them. Their drawings are personal projections reflecting what is happening in their innermost being.

The book, *Drawing With Children*, by Mona Brooks is a very good guide for parents and school teachers. In this book there is a course called, "Enhancing Creative Capacity for Children and Adults." Frequent interaction with a variety of materials and art forms is very helpful for anyone who is trying to balance stress in their life. Needlework, knitting, sewing, painting, and sculpting help keep stress to a minimum. Woodworking and building with blocks can develop a structural art talent that may develop into a career. Remember to teach children to respect their environment and develop good organizational skills, by making sure they clean up when finished, thoroughly putting everything in its proper place so it is available for the next joyful experience.

Sports: Individual vs. Team—Karate, gymnastics, and swimming can be very helpful in developing a mind/body connection. They increase self-discipline if taught by a knowledgeable instructor who understands children with special needs like ADD/ADHD or Autism.

It has also been written in many parenting books that children who have many stressors in their lives succeed when developing their skills and talents in individual or partner type sports and activities. Children who have difficulty organizing, writing, or staying focused, seem to enjoy sports such as swimming, martial arts, dance, gymnastics, horseback riding, and wall climbing. Tennis, ping-pong, billiards, and horseshoes can be great helps in developing eye-hand coordination and other visual processing skills. Although, when considering swimming, remember that chlorine is toxic and many children have a sensitivity to it.

Light Therapy—One cause for depression can be improper lighting and lack of exposure to sunshine. SunBox™ light units are to our knowledge, the only units approved for use at the National Institute of Mental Health in Bethesda, Maryland. SunBox™ light units are clinically tested and proven effective, exceeding hospital and government safety standards. This company is listed in our appendix section. Light Therapy is a simple procedure of exposing oneself to sunlight or artificial sunlight for a certain period of time.

Vibratory Frequency and the Senses: Music Therapy— What is absorbed into one's mind through the sense of hearing needs careful consideration. Sounds affect our innermost being and greatly influence our emotional status. Sudden, loud, harsh, shrill, disharmonic, or pounding sounds are harmful in many ways and can affect a person's mood instantly. Conversely, rhythmic or melodious sounds, such as classical music, calm the spirit and help integrate the right and left brain hemispheres. This integration creates a more balanced human being. We are

Whole Child Institute

vibratory beings highly affected by the vibrations of everything in our world. Gifted and talented people with very high IQ's tend to be more sensitive to touch, smell, sounds, and sights than others. Many individuals who have learning and/or behavioral challenges are also very bright and highly sensitive to the world around them. It is of utmost importance for them to experience the greatest possible sensory inputs of high vibratory frequency. These would be things like colors of the rainbow, the metal gold, gemstones, or classical music. Sounds like chimes and xylophones, or musical instruments can be used to create pleasant sounds. Silence is also a very supportive experience to the senses. It can be extremely calming and adds to balance.

Essential Oils—Organic, high-quality essential oils bring balance to the body with their antibacterial, antifungal, and antiviral properties. They also can neutralize chemicals. It is important to be aware that not all essential oils are as effective as others. Essential oils are the life force, or essentially, the blood of a plant. Everything in our environment, including essential oils, has an electrical frequency. The flow of this frequency is measured in hertz. In the book, *The Body Electric,* Robert O. Becker, M.D., validates the electrical frequency of the human body and substances in our environment. In terms of hertz measurement, the goal for health in the human body is to keep the frequency of electrical energy as high as possible. When illness, whether it be mental, emotional, or physical, lowers the body's energy level, essential oils can be used effectively to raise its electrical frequency.

Some facts to consider...

- Healthy body—62-78 hertz
- Disease begins—58 hertz
- Processed/canned foods—0 hertz
- Fresh produce—up to 15 hertz
- Essential oils—52-322 hertz

An advantage to using essential oils for children, is that they are applied topically. There are no pills or capsules to try to get down the throat of a challenging child. One merely puts a few drops on the palms, rubs them together, and inhales the aroma. The oils can also be used in the bath, or they can be rubbed on meridian points on any area of the body needing healing. According to aromacologist Dr. Gary Young, N.D., "Research shows that essential oils have the highest frequency of any substance known to man, creating an environment in which disease, bacteria, viruses and fungus cannot live." Dr. Young believes that the chemistry and frequency of essential oils have the ability to help man maintain the optimal electrical frequency to the extent that disease cannot exist. Furthermore, he feels it is imperative that the public understand that the popularity of essential oils is causing some people to place money before quality. He warns of cheap essential oils that are not organic and that do not carry the frequency and healing properties of a quality product.

Families dealing with children who are challenging face many obstacles in finding professional help, interacting with school staff, and managing their lives around these challenges. Here we have included a few tips we have picked up over the years that we hope you will find helpful.

Move On—Beware of feeling "stuck" with a practitioner, health care provider, or therapist. Change is often very challenging and can be stressful in and of itself, especially when it comes to the professionals who care for ones family. Be courageous and try a new service provider when results or interactions with a certain provider are not really meeting your needs. Be willing to ask other parents for a recommendation. Follow your logic, intuition, and innermost feelings when it comes to the final decision. For instance, if you are strongly opposed to using antibiotics for ear infections and a doctor prescribes an antibiotic for an ear infection, do what you feel is best. There are many other ways to treat infections holistically (taking into consideration the whole body and how it functions, rather than merely addressing symptoms). Take charge, Mom and Dad, and do your homework diligently!

Test Taking—Many students can be very successful without feeling stress over daily assignments and processing work during class time. However, when they are faced with taking a test, they may be overcome with stress. This is often referred to as test anxiety. Drinking an ample amount of pure water, and practicing test taking ahead of time (at home in a relaxed environment) can be helpful in releasing the anxiety associated with test taking. The Kumon Math & Reading Program also helps students overcome test anxiety.

Anger/Forgiveness—"Anger can be dangerous to your health." states Redford Williams, M.D. in his book, *Anger Kills*. Williams is a behavioral scientist at Duke University. He is a Professor of Psychology and an Associate Professor of Medicine. In his book, he documents health hazards of hostility such as diabetes and offers practical antidotes. At the Whole Child Institute, we teach parents and children to focus on the positive aspects of a situation. We encourage each family to share the good things about their day. We encourage the exploration of angry feelings and how to take responsibility for one's own feelings. Blaming others prevents taking responsibility for one's actions. Anger can block how much a person is really hurting and can be used as a defense for feeling frustrated, afraid, ashamed, or lonely. By putting aside anger, one can identify the hurt feelings. Finding ways to soothe our hurt feelings helps us to lessen anger. We must remember that anger is only one of many choices we have when dealing with our circumstances.

At the Whole Child Institute we teach children that it is not okay if someone hurts them or takes a toy away from them. Many children will say, "That's okay!," when another child tells them they are sorry after hurting them. We believe a more accurate response would be, "I forgive you," because it is not okay if another person hurts you.

Planning and Time Management—"Fail to Plan, Plan to Fail." Taking some quiet time out of ones busy life to actually plan an ideal day saves so much time and energy in the long run. It takes good planning in order to create an ideal school day, the perfect summer day, a smooth weekend, or a great holiday. Children learn time management and goal setting best by the example of adults in their lives. Teachers, childcare providers, moms, and dads all know that chaos can so quickly prevail when there is no plan in place. It is up to the adults in a child's world to help him learn to balance his time and energy on a daily basis. From very early on, a child can see calendars and daily planning guides as helpful when it comes to balancing a busy lifestyle. Consider helping your child use a personal calendar or time management system to help plan her day. Anything important needs to be scheduled in order for it to get done in a calm, harmonious manner. Even the simple task of drinking water may need to be scheduled. You can set it to go off once every hour to remind him to drink a cup of water. This practice will help a child learn how fast time goes by and he will begin to understand the progression and concept of time.

Daily rituals are an important part of time management. We suggest morning prayers, dedicating the day to God and asking for His guidance and protection, then bedtime prayers for expressing gratitude for what was learned, enjoyed, and experienced that day. Children learn to replace anger with forgiveness when they have a nightly ritual of prayer asking God to forgive them for anything or anyway they may have hurt someone. Children also need to understand the concept of praying without ceasing (that constant link to their creator.) A short simple ritual of asking a blessing for food and giving thanks, also instills important values in a child.

Prayer and water drinking are just two examples of daily rituals that may need scheduling in order to keep daily life in balance.

There are also school and extra-curricular activities, homework, socialization times, meals, and personal hygiene. Forecasting, or telling a child what is going to happen and when it will happen, is extremely helpful for keeping family life balanced. It makes a child feel secure and helps to keep him emotionally and mentally stable. It has proven to be a vital part of success in the life of a child dealing with ADD/ADHD or emotional challenges. In particular, transitions of any sort are very challenging for these children. When a change in routine is necessary let a child know that you will be there to help her handle the situation. Planning is the key to bringing balance into our lives on a daily basis.

What is Aspartame (NutraSweet/Equal™)?

Phenylalanine—neurotoxin
Methanol—breaks down into Formaldehyde (embalming fluid). Damaging to the eyes, liver, brain, and other organs of the body.
Formic Acid—ant sting venom
Diketopiperazine (DKP)—nitrosated in the digestive process, thus creating a potentially carcinogenic condition.
Aspartic Acid—**(40%)** least dangerous component, yet it changed DNA in third generation laboratory pups who were born, unlike their parents, morbidly obese and sexually dysfunctional.
Brain Scientists at MIT and others say the components of Aspartame are capable of crossing the blood brain barrier.

PKU (phenylketonuria) "An inherited disorder caused by a lack of an enzyme necessary to convert the amino acid phenylalanine into another amino acid, tyrosine, so that excesses can be eliminated from the body. A buildup of excess phenylalanine in the blood can lead to neurological disturbances and mental retardation." James Balch, M.D. *Prescription For Healing—Second Edition. A practical A-Z reference to drug-free remedies using vitamins, minerals, herbs and food supplements.* Aspartame puts those with PKU or carries of PKU at great risk.

For more information about Aspartame, contact the Aspartame Consumer Safety Network: 1-800-969-6050.

Vaccines—The First International Public Conference on Vaccination was held in September 1997 in Alexandria, VA. Experts met to talk about how vaccines cause injury, chronic illness and even death. Topics included vaccines and infant death, biological mechanisms of vaccine injury and vaccine reaction to blood tests, vaccines and learning disabilities, measles vaccine, hepatitis B–vaccine injuries, viral vaccines and chromosome damage, vaccine administration combined with other hazardous exposures, vaccine regulation, and polio vaccine contamination. The concurring view point by no means opposed childhood vaccines, but virtually all of the participants agreed that a headlong rush into current vaccine programs without adequate safety screening was foolish.

As noted, in the October 1998 Townsend Letter for Doctors & Patients in an article by Harold E. Buttram, M.D., entitled The National Childhood Vaccine Injury Act–A Critique–, "Theoretically there are three major areas in which current childhood vaccines may injure the child:

1. The dysregulation, crippling, or stunting of children's immune systems.
2. The induction of autoimmune reactions which react adversely on organ systems, such as the brain.
3. The contamination of live-virus vaccines with potentially injurious foreign viruses.

Dr. Buttram states, "There is at present an ominous trend of deteriorating health among large segments of American children. As one example there is a rapid increase in the incidence, severity, and death rate from asthma. Developmental delay, children requiring special education, and autism are rapidly increasing in incidence. The incidence of autism is now soaring with an estimated incidence of 250,000 autistic children in America, which represents a 10 to 15 times increase in the past 50 or so years, a time period concurrent with mass childhood vaccine programs. These figures are the estimates of Bernard Rimland, Ph.D., internationally recognized as a leading authority on autism, based on more than 40 years of experience in the field. Dr. Rimland has publicly stated his opinion that vaccines are one of the major contributory causes of the increasing incidence of autism. The causative relation between vaccines and these adverse health trends can neither be proven nor disproven at present, largely due to the inadequacies of basic safety testing for the vaccines. However, it should be remembered that the children themselves will be our ultimate judges in future years, should we fail them at this critical juncture."

Parents often make the decision to vaccinate based on pressure from the "system" rather than getting information on both sides of the issue. It is vital that parents get cutting edge information and support if they choose not to vaccinate their children. There is an excellent video available and abundant written information to help parents choose and withstand the pressures of society when it comes to vaccination. Barbara Loe Fisher is the editor of a good bi-monthly publication entitled, *The Vaccine Reaction: "When it happens to you or your child, the risks are 100%."* Barbara writes, "Knowledge is power." You can find out what the Center for Disease Control is saying by visiting the CDC internet page at http://www.CDC.gov.nip or NIC website at www.909shot.com or write them at 512 W. Maple Ave., #206, Vienna, VA 22180 or call 1-800-909-SHOT.

At the Whole Child Institute we feel parents should get accurate information so they can make informed decisions. Children with compromised immune systems are not always the best candidates for vaccines. We caution parents to get all of the facts. Dr. Buttram, M.D. can be contacted at (215) 536-1890.

Chapter Twenty

Grace discovered early on that Paul's respiratory problems were directly related to a milk allergy. As he developed he suffered from asthma even when dairy was eliminated from his diet. This prompted her to seek further assessments concerning food allergies and sensitivities. Paul's Sunday school teacher happened to be a staff member at the Whole Child Institute. One day after class, she shared information about the Whole Child Institute and what a whole child assessment could do to help Paul's mother fit together the pieces of his behavioral puzzle. Her story begins with Paul at age eight.

"I knew I had a child with high energy and some behavioral issues who is very smart and has health concerns. My problem was, I just didn't understand the interconnectedness of all these factors and where I could go for help. I am a Physical Therapist and I understand how the body can heal itself. I was really not interested in being coerced by the school or medical people to use drugs or for that matter, use traditional labeling for Paul. I knew preventive intervention is what I was really seeking and was so grateful when I found out about the Whole Child Institute and the informal whole child assessment. It was spring and second grade was coming to an end. Paul's teacher had expressed some concerns to me about Paul's social skills, his difficulty with staying on task, and other behaviors that were disruptive in the classroom. I decided to take Paul to the Whole Child Institute. After his assessment it was suggested that I schedule a meeting with the teachers and principal from his private school, plus a psychologist from the public school district. The psychologist was invited by Paul's teacher and had my approval to make some classroom observations. A staff member from the Institute accompanied me to the school meeting. She heard information that was shared which I didn't grasp and was able to interpret it for me; I really appreciated that. With her help I was able to understand the ramifications of decisions that were made at the meeting. She helped me to see that the district was not going to evaluate my son for ADD, because they felt it was a medical diagnosis. I would be responsible financially and otherwise to get this done. This meeting taught me a very big lesson; getting an advocate for school meetings and developing ones own advocacy skills can help tremendously!

PACER Center, a parent rights advocacy organization, located in Minneapolis, Minnesota, was sponsoring a presentation on ADD by a man named Jerry Mills. A Whole Child Institute staff member suggested I attend. I was so glad I went to hear Jerry's message. He really touched my heart. What he shared helped me realize that my brother probably had ADD and that I was inclined towards ADHD considering the way I go, go, go, and never stop. I realized that some of the ways I had been interacting with Paul were incorrect for a child with ADD and I began to look at Paul in a different light. What I learned helped me to gain control over various situations and deal with him in a way that was much better for both of us. I started acknowledging his feelings and frustrations with unconditional love and expressed acceptance of who he was. Our relationship is gradually improving since I became aware of these facts.

The whole child assessment helped me put many of the pieces of this very complex puzzle together. I learned about a great variety of factors that contributed to my son's present status. I knew he was extremely bright, but I didn't have a clue how many other factors influence his performance in the school setting such as environmental toxicity, food sensitivities, bio-chemical imbalances, fluorescent lighting, learning styles, learning byte, and feelings about various elements of his daily life. The assessment information helped me get a grip on the totality of what I was really dealing with.

Kumon Math was recommended to help bring his math skills up to his ability level. Paul briefly attended a Kumon Center and was also able to take advantage of some short term Learning Gap Therapy through the Whole Child Institute. He learned body-brain connection exercises in order to slow down his brain. Eventually he became more accurate in academics and more in control behaviorally. The Institute had been following the research on a certain antioxidant supplement and I decided to try it with Paul. When I ran out, I switched to a cheaper brand, and symptoms that had disappeared while on the first brand, reappeared. It only took four days for me to see the difference, the inexpensive supplement was not working and I quickly went back to the initial supplement. I immediately noticed a marked improvement in his behavior and overall health. His asthma and allergy problems decreased and he became a calmer, more compliant child. He is doing better at dealing with authority; his self-control has increased greatly. It has been brought to my attention that school in general is going much better, but he still has problems being in some group situations.

Upon the recommendation of the Whole Child Institute, I also attended a lecture by a certified clinical nutritionist. Her confirmation of things I already knew was comforting. I realized that she understood a lot about ADD and treating it by looking beyond symptoms. I made an appointment with her and was amazed at what she found.

Because Paul's family history includes alcoholism in his biological father, he has problems with digestion as the result of a lack of amino acids and a B-vitamin. Heavy metals and environmental poisons were too excessive and were causing some of his problems. This nutritionist believes that for a child, everyday is significant and it's vitally important that children get proper nutrition every day so that they have a good foundation for proper growth and development.

We began a cleansing program because of the history of alcoholism in the family. The nutritionist explained that Paul had excess chemicals in his body, which caused him to have parasites, this in turn caused him to have Candida (or yeast) in his system. First we cleansed the excess chemicals from his body using antioxidants and then we worked on the parasite problem. After the parasites were cleaned out, we then took care of the Candida. By this time, Paul was almost ten years old; he had finished his detoxification regime and was following a specific nutritional program designed by his clinical nutritionist. He is now able to digest what he eats, assimilating nutrients from his food more efficiently. He sees her now on a maintenance basis. I no longer need to spend the extra time or money (it was expensive, but worth every penny) taking him to the clinical nutritionist. I am so grateful that I was led to all the various resources suggested by the Whole Child Institute, and I would love to create a billboard with our clinical nutritionists favorite saying, PAY NOW, OR PAY MORE LATER!

Although it was challenging to pay for some of these resources, I will never be sorry to have sacrificed temporarily, while Paul was still young, in order to make a difference, which will last him a lifetime.

During the cleansing process, we also worked at cleaning up his environment of as many chemical pollutants as possible. I read all about how this is done in Dr. Crook's book, *Help for the Hyperactive Child*. We also made lifestyle changes to reduce the stress in Paul's life. Stress is a major immune system antagonizer. By forcing him to fit into my very active lifestyle, Paul was getting an overdose of stimulation that was very unhealthy.

I learned that in helping my child decrease his aggressive and hyperactive behavior, I needed to control his television viewing. While reading Dr. Crook's book, *Help for the Hyperactive* Child, I came face-to-face with the reality of how much television influenced my son's behavior, especially watching programs like Beavis and Butthead, The Simpson's, and Power Rangers. TV ads promoting cereals and other nutritionally deficient foods containing sugar, food coloring and additives were also making it difficult for me to get his cooperation in eating healthy foods. I began to consider that when he is watching television, he is not getting much exercise or practice in social skills.

At the beginning of Paul's third grade year, I was able to meet with his principal and his teacher in order to tell them of his assets and ways they could help him focus. I brought Jerry Mill's booklet along because it has specific instructions for teachers. Paul's teacher has been very good about working with him and me. His previous teacher would interrupt class discussions and draw attention to Paul's excessive movements. This was very disruptive to the whole class and diverted their attention from the lesson onto Paul. His current teacher noted that for a child with ADD, the worst thing you can do is to point out their lack of attention in front of the class. His present teacher found that if she ignores his movements and begins to draw him into the discussions, his movements decrease and the other children are not distracted by him at all. These tactics of hers were a major breakthrough that I plan to share with future teachers. She also used a reward system that really worked well for Paul. Other teachers have had him stay in during recess a few times because of his behavior, but taking away a child's recess, especially one with behavioral issues, is one of the worst forms of intervention a teacher can use. Children with learning or behavioral issues need frequent activity breaks for fresh air, sunlight, water, and social integration in order to maintain a sense of balance throughout the school day. His first report card this year reflected the best behavior he's ever had in school.

I feel that my son's whole child assessment was the beginning of a long road, which is full of resources to help Paul reach his full potential. Paul is very creative and has a lot to offer. I believe he will succeed in life with help and understanding support from the adults around him. Thanks to the Whole Child Institute, Paul's teachers and I are now better equipped to offer that support."

At the Whole Child Institute we recognize that raising a child who is challenging is extremely difficult. It takes a lot of resources and a variety of preventive interventions to turn around their less desirable characteristics. We are encouraged when we can make a difference in the lives of children like Paul.

Remember to take time to interact with your child. When dealing with children who are challenging, it is good to keep in mind that...

Yesterday is history,

Tomorrow's a mystery,

Today is a gift,

That's why we call it the present!

Chapter Twenty-one

Camye, at the tender age of five and a half, was able to overcome dyslexia and learn to read. Her mother, Sharon, brought her to the Whole Child Institute because she saw how Camye's personality and dyslexic symptoms mirrored her own childhood. Sharon sought early intervention for Camye so she wouldn't have to struggle in school. Sharon had struggled in school until twelfth grade when she developed strategies to compensate for her own dyslexia. Her story starts with Camye in utero.

"When I was pregnant with my daughter Camye, I had fibrous tumors in my placenta. Over half of my womb was placenta, leaving Camye in breech position and crammed into one area. My doctor didn't think I would be able to deliver her vaginally, so I was planning on having a C-section. She did manage to turn and I was able to deliver her normally.

Even though Camye was six pounds eight ounces she had problems holding her temperature up to normal. She would get really cold. I had to keep a hat on her and keep her bundled up even though it was the end of May. By two months of age, her body was finally able to regulate a normal temperature. She also had nutritional jaundice and I was told to feed her every four hours for the first two weeks. Although she slept through the night right from the beginning, the doctor who diagnosed her jaundice said I should wake her up to feed her. After two weeks, her doctor said she was fine, so I stopped waking her up and she slept full nights. She was a very good baby. She hardly ever cried. She would just start to wiggle a little bit when she was uncomfortable or needed to eat. I did notice, however, that she was very sensitive to loud noises. She never wanted anyone to touch her hair, but by her fourth birthday I was able to put her hair up in a pony tail. Now I realize she was dealing with some sensory integration processing problems.

When Camye was a year old, I started reading to her every night. By the age of two, she had three books that she could 'read' to me any time. At two-and-a-half she had about twenty books memorized. Her seven year-old cousin, who was struggling to learn to read, was frustrated because she thought Camye could read. She was greatly relieved when I told her that Camye wasn't actually reading, but that she had only memorized her books. By the time she was three, Camye was begging me to teach her how to read. She was angry that she didn't know all of her books. I spoke with some teachers in the local school district and some preschools and they all said they would not teach her to read because it was not age appropriate. Camye would actually cry at night begging me to teach her to read. I had no one to turn to, and I didn't know what I could do to teach her, so I just read to her more.

When she was three I found a very good preschool where a lady worked in her own home providing care for a few children ages two to four years old. Camye was kept very busy. She was happy there and very stimulated.

Camye's behavior was always at one extreme or the other. I noticed that she was either going a hundred miles per hour or if I held her still for a few minutes, she would fall asleep. There was no in between.

At the age of one year, I gave her some Dairy Queen soft-serve ice cream. It was just one small scoop off the top of a single serving, she didn't even eat the whole thing. I noticed she became very anxious, as if she couldn't stand being inside of herself. The sugar in the icecream really stressed her out. I never gave her much sugar in the first place, because our family has a history of diabetes and hypoglycemia, but at that point, I decided to take her off of all foods containing refined sugar.

People would tell me it's normal for kids to be a little hyper. I would say, 'No, it's not that Camye's hyper; she's anxious.' People wouldn't believe me when I said that she was highly affected by sugar. They would blame it on her being my first child, and my inexperience as a parent. Camye would just lose control! By age two I taught her the word 'control'. Whenever she was out of control I would say, 'Camye, you're out of control.' Sometimes I would ask her, 'Do you feel ornery?' 'If you feel ornery, then you have to go and be by yourself for awhile.' Ornery meant that she felt she would do something mean or was getting anxious. Sometimes when she was out of control or 'ornery' she would scream out, just a quick burst. I have now learned that this can be a sign of autism.

When she was three, I became pregnant with her younger sister Marissa and was not able to spend as much time with Camye because I would fall asleep before she would. Her sister was born when she was four years old. I had to move Camye from her preschool, because they wouldn't take babies. I put her in a daycare that would take her sister as well. Her new provider was a neighbor and I knew her from our church. Camye started getting into trouble in her new daycare setting within the first few weeks. I would pick her up day after day and hear stories about how naughty Camye had been. I spoke with her caregiver and she agreed to give Camye more attention, but she also had two babies to care for. The situation just became worse. One day, Camye was very out of control and her caregiver called and asked me to come and pick her up. She seemed over tired when I picked her up so I let her rest for most of the day. Her behavior always seemed to escalate when she was tired; that is when the 'orneries' would start. About a week later, I came to pick her up after work and her caregiver said that Camye was out of control again. I asked when it had started and she said, 'About nine o'clock this morning. I didn't want to call you again, because I knew you had to work.' When I asked her what had happened, she answered, 'I couldn't go in the room where she is now, I couldn't get her to come out, I didn't know what to do with her, so I left her in there all day. If you go in there now, she will probably think it's lunch time, because she hasn't even had lunch yet.' It was four o'clock in the afternoon! When Camye saw me she told me she was hungry; she did want to know if it was lunch time and asked if I had come to have lunch with her. She was very calm, and playing very nicely on the floor. I said, 'No honey, it's four o'clock and we're going to go home.' She was very confused, she didn't understand the concept of time. She couldn't tell whether five minutes or five hours had gone by. I cried all the way home after picking Camye and Marissa up. I knew I had to make a change and she couldn't stay there any longer. I visited various preschools and daycares. I was not happy with the traditional ones. I found one preschool that was one of the first ones in the state of Minnesota, called Tutor Time. It is a very good program. They have accredited teachers, and it is a preschool, not a daycare center. They take infants and had an opening for both of my girls. I was able to enroll Camye and Marissa right away. They loved it! When I would pick them up, Camye's face would be glowing. I could tell she was busy all day long, doing very positive things, and she was getting very positive teaching. She was no longer getting in trouble everyday, she was having fun. The teachers were saying that she was a delight to have in their class. She would finish the things that they gave her to do, then she would get up and help the other kids. She would be a helper for half of her day. She has always enjoyed being a helper. I finally felt that everything was going well.

When Camye was learning to write, I started watching for reversals because we have a history of dyslexia in my family. During her kindergarten screening I was told she didn't have very good fine motor skills. She is left-handed, so I felt that is what affected her writing skills and the test administrators did too. I asked about the letter and number reversals and I was told that it was pretty normal for her age. She was only three-and-a-half. I was told this usually clears up around age five. Camye would write her entire name backwards, E first, then M, Y, A, C and each letter would also be backwards. She couldn't tell the difference between b/d, m/w, p/q or a five and a two. Those were very hard for her. Since dyslexia runs in my family, I wanted to have her tested or get her some therapy for it, so that when she started school she wouldn't experience the problems my brother and I had gone through in school.

When she was five, Camye was still confusing her letters. People would tell me that this was normal for her age. After my own experience with dyslexia, I knew it was unfair for any child to have to deal with these symptoms at any age. My sister had discovered the Whole Child Institute. I thought I'd bring Camye in for a Whole Child Assessment. They tested her and it was discovered that she was probably dealing with Dyslexia, ADD, High-Functioning Autism, and had an I.Q. in the gifted range. She also most likely had Dyscalculia, which is a problem with numbers and mathematics. I realized that I was not the only person who thought that some of the things she did were abnormal. Finally, someone understood and did not try to discount what I had noticed in Camye.

Just before Camye started kindergarten, she began Kumon instruction. In the morning she would go to the kindergarten program at Tutor Time. In the afternoon, she was in the school district kindergarten and after school, she would do Kumon. She would go to the Kumon Center twice a week and every day she had math and reading worksheets to do. It started to be too much for her, and she began sleeping for up to twelve hours each night. She would go to sleep between five to seven o'clock in the evening and wake up at six or seven o'clock the next morning.

I spoke with the learning specialist at the Whole Child Institute, thinking that maybe Camye was getting too much stimulation. It was as if her brain was exhausted. She wasn't making any progress in Kumon and was struggling with all of her schoolwork. Finally, I hired a special education teacher from the Whole Child Institute to come to my home and do homeschooling with Camye and Marissa. After experiencing the Learning Gap Therapy, Camye rarely ever turned a letter. If she did she would catch herself. She could read real words and sentences. She was able to sound them out using a technique from the Whole Child Institute that breaks through learning barriers she and many other children have.

During this time, I was concerned about a five-hour trip that we had to take in the car. I knew how hard it was for Camye to 'keep it together' when she was tired, not eating well, and off her schedule, and I was not looking forward to it. Since we had started with the Whole Child Institute, she was on vitamin supplements and also doing Kumon, so I thought that would keep her in check. She could do a little homework everyday to keep her mind busy. We were going to have to eat out though, and that's what I feared the most. Normally, I would spend the whole time at restaurants telling Camye to sit down, or come back, or stay on her chair, or to eat. I was feeling exhausted even before I left, but we had to make this trip. We left on a Friday, and by Sunday at brunch I had tears in my eyes. Of the five meals we ate out, I did not have to tell Camye once to sit down, get back in her chair or not to walk around the table. I could talk to her and enjoy her company. I sat there thinking that this is the little girl that I knew she could be. A few months earlier we had been out to dinner and I had seen a couple sitting with their children who were about five and seven years old. They just sat there and had a nice dinner. I thought it would be so nice just to sit and have a whole dinner without having to tell Camye to sit still. Now, two months later, I was doing just that.

Camye may have 'an episode' during the week where she screams, but she gets herself back under control within minutes. For the most part, she is able to control herself through out an entire day. She can handle boredom, which she could not do before. She now understands the concept and progression of time. The Institute has worked with her to understand minutes, hours, time of day, days of the week, and months of the year. She understands all of this, within only two months of working with her special education teacher on a daily basis.

Camye would not be where she is today if it had not been for the Whole Child Institute, helping her and coaching me so that I can continue the training. It has taken two months to deal with Camye's emotional and behavioral situations. Applying what I have learned has resulted in a sweet little girl who had been locked up inside and is now out for everyone to see. The time, money, and energy I have invested in my daughter was well worth it."

At only six years of age, Camye is now able to advocate for herself and tell others what she needs and how she learns. She is also able to teach what she has learned to other children including her younger sister Marissa.

Chapter Twenty-two

This chapter was written in order to assist those coming in contact with families dealing with children who are challenging, i.e. teachers, extra-curricular activity instructors and coaches, pastors, scout leaders, lawmakers, law enforcement officers, probation officers, etc. These people can help by connecting families with resources such as the Whole Child Institute, and those listed in the appendix section of this book.

Other Ways To Help

Listening
Empathizing
Educating
Modeling
Mentoring
Team Work
Third Party Influence
Sharing Brochures/Pamphlets
Helping With Phone Calls
Connecting/Re-connecting

The Whole Child Institute creates a sanctuary for families with children who for a variety of reasons are challenging. People who share a common direction create a sense of community. Like geese, these families begin to travel on the thrust of one another. Science has discovered that geese flying in a V-formation have seventy-one percent greater flying range than if each bird flew on its own. In the V-formation each bird flaps its wings creating an uplift for the bird immediately following. When a goose falls out of formation, it suddenly feels the drag and resistance of trying to go it alone and quickly gets back into formation to take advantage of the lifting power of the bird in front. Parents soon realize they need to stay close to other parents who are headed in the same direction; obtaining healthy ways of dealing with their child's challenges.

When a goose gets sick or wounded and falls out of formation, two other geese fall out with that goose and follow it down to lend help and protection. They stay with the fallen goose until it is able to fly or until it dies and only then will they launch out on their own or with another formation to catch up with their group. Mary Topero and Linda Vettrus, co-founders of the Whole Child Institute concentrated on empowering parents of challenging children and seeing themselves as promoting the "sense of the goose" teaching families to stand by each other for help and support.

There is no magic formula other than doing the best we can! Families with children who deal with major challenges are generally stressed to the max and are doing the best they can, not the best they would like to be doing. Therefore, they deal with a lot of guilt. Helping these families realize that they are doing their best and letting them know that you are there to support them will allow them to move towards doing the best they would like to be doing.

All of us have a life-long need for acceptance and positive strokes from others. The feeling of isolation is painful. You can help by connecting these families with various organizations and resources, preferably free with little time committment. Flexibility is also key. Drop-in support groups are usually best.

The best advice is advice that works for you. Therefore, unless you are sharing from your own experience, advice quickly turns into insult. Becky Kajander, C.P.N.P., M.P.H. in her book, *Living with ADHD—a practical guide to coping with ADHD* gives a list of basics for frazzled parents.

1. Ask for help from friends and relatives
2. Get help from professionals
3. Join a support group
4. Stay in close contact with your child's teachers
5. Remember to enjoy your child.

"By nature, children with ADHD are impulsive. They have a hard time seeing another person's point of view, they tend to blame others for their problems, and they don't always take responsibility well."

—Becky Kajander, C.P.N.P., M.P.H.

Understanding behavior is the key to managing a relationship with a child dealing with ADHD and any other challenges.

**Suggested viewing for better understanding
of parents in crisis...**

Videos: Lorenzo's Oil
House of Cards
First Do No Harm

Suggested reading for understanding ADD/ADHD...

Putting On The Brakes,
by Patricia Quinn, M.D. & Judith M. Stern, M.D.

You Mean I'm Not Lazy, Crazy or Stupid?,
by Kate Kelly & Peggy Ramundo

**Suggested reading for understanding the importance
of keeping a healthy intestinal track...**

Help For The Hyperactive Child, by Dr. William Crook, M.D.

People First Language

While walking down the street with your child, you see a man using crutches due to a broken leg. Your child says, "Look Dad, there's a broken-legged man." What would you say to your child? You would probably correct your child's grammar by saying, "No honey, that's a <u>man</u> <u>with</u> a broken leg."

A man <u>dealing with</u> a broken leg.

A child <u>dealing with</u> Down's Syndrome or

a child <u>with</u> Down's Syndrome.

A person <u>dealing with</u> autism or

a person <u>with</u> autism.

A person dealing <u>with</u> learning challenges or

a person <u>with</u> learning differences.

Not...

An Autistic person.

An ADHD child.

A Dyslexic child.

A Learning Disabled child.

A handicapped person.

At the Whole Child Institute we believe in using people first language. We believe in stating the <u>person</u> <u>first</u>, then what they are <u>dealing</u> <u>with</u>, not what they are.

Example: <u>A child,</u> <u>dealing with</u> <u>ADHD</u>.
not
an ADHD child.

<u>This concept was first introduced by</u>
<u>L.D.M., Learning Disabilities of Minneso</u>ta.

Please help us
promote
the use of...

People First Language

Puzzle Pieces

Things for parents to do while putting the pieces together!

- Give TLC (tender loving care) to the major caregiver.
- Drink sufficient amounts of pure water throughout each day.
- Deep breathing accompanied by music
- Think about good nutrition when choosing what to buy, eat or drink.
- Slow down and enjoy the simple pleasures of life.
- Learn the value of aromatherapy.
- Explore art and music therapy for your child.
- Consider any elements of Occupational Therapy that you might incorporate into your child's daily activities.
- Look at healthy images in pictures and movies as much as possible.
- Wear uplifting vibrant colored clothing.
- Put your attention on what it is you really desire.
- Do Brain-Gym™ exercises with your child.
- Feed your body and brain the specific nutrients needed in order to attain optimum health.
- Do at least one kind deed daily!
- Read something that is uplifting, educational, inspiring or encouraging—a little bit everyday, on a regular basis and share it with your child.
- Give positive affirmations and messages to your children—catch them doing something right.
- Encourage, individual and family, community service activities.
- Realize that flexibility is the key to sanity!

- Forecast routines, schedules, events, and activities as much as possible, as well as any changes to them.
- Organize yourself, household, and family to the best of your ability.
- Ask for help from neighbors, church members, clergy, friends, teachers, school-home liaison workers, family resource workers, school social workers, counselors, coaches, teachers, your child's peers and their parents, relatives, advocacy professionals, psychologists, nurse practitioners, family doctor or behavioral pediatrician, YMCA Staff, etc. **In other words, reach out for help!**

A Parent's Report Card

What Kinds of Grades Are You Getting?

1. I monitor T.V. and computer use.
2. I connect with my child's school on a regular basis.
3. I help my child choose appropriate friends.
4. I find ways to help myself.
5. I take time for myself
6. I encourage individual sports and activities.
7. I make sure others have important information about working with my child.
8. I motivate my child to drink lots of pure water all day long.
9. I provide healthy food for my family.
10. I am loving while providing discipline, especially in front of others.
11. I forecast possible changes in routine and my expectations for the day/week.
12. I model responding with "I forgive you," to an apology rather than just saying, "Oh, that's OK."
13. I provide a daily rest time or "down time" for my child as well as for myself.

Grading: One point for each yes.

11-13 pts. = A   8-10 pts. = B   5-7 pts. = C

Less than 5 = Needs Improvement

_____Linda Vettrus_____
___Director of the Whole Child Institute___

Credentials:

- Bachelor of Science Degree in Special Education, St. Cloud State University, 1979
- World Relief MN—Sponsorship Developer/Public Relations
- Former Educational Consultant for Discovery Toys
- Homeschool Educator
- Developed Therapeutic Preparatory Exercises for Writing Road To Reading
- Discovered Patterned Learners
- Co-founder and Director of the Whole Child Institute
- Chair of MN Children's EBD Steering Committee and Advisory Group

Outline of experiences working with children:

- Special Education Teacher (K-12)
- ESL (English as a Second Language) Tutor
- BSF Children's Program—Leader and Assistant to Supervisor
- Living Skills Educator—Group Homes for Developmentally Disabled
- SILS Program Coordinator—Educator for Independent Living Skills
- Bloomington Park and Recreation—Special Needs Summer Program

Book: Challenging Children—A Puzzle To Be SOLVED: Stories from Parent's Who Were Empowered by the WCI, foreword by Keith W. Sehnert, M.D.

Outline of content:

A reference guide that reveals the importance of early intervention and explores the relationship between nutrition and body brain connection, advocacy and survival, toxicity and health, movement and learning. These stories were written by parents who have received helpful guidance from the Whole Child Institute.

"These stories were compiled in order to help parents and professionals explore various cause and core reasons why we are seeing such an increase of high needs children today."

—Dr. Keith Sehnert, M.D.

Field Experiences

- Taught various classes for community education, Family Support Network (The Home of Parents Anonymous of MN), MN School of Professional Psychology, Barnes and Noble, Whole Foods Market, etc.

- Magazine Articles and Television/Radio Interviews

- LDM (Learning Disabilities of MN) Roundtable Discussion Leader

Other courses, besides degreed educational courses, Linda Vettrus has taken that relate to the whole child concept…

Workshops/Conferences:

- Institute for Adolescents with Behavioral Disorders and The Police Institute
- John Taylor

- Twin Cities Autism Society Conferences
- Associates 2000 Conferences
- MACMH Conferences (MN Association for Children's Mental Health)
- Health Seminars
- New Visions School—Power Packed Learning: with Dr. Lyelle Palmer

The Whole Child Institute offers:

Assessments which empower parents and professionals to work at the cause and core level with children who, for a variety of reasons, are challenging. A whole child assessment utilizes a very simple but profound technique which provides cause and core information resulting in an action plan that can be used as a school advocacy tool and improve the quality of family life.

The goal of the action plan is to bring together the pieces of the puzzle that assist an individual to blossom forth experiencing a body/brain connection that brings achievement up to ability level. The assessment includes various puzzle pieces such as, learning styles, seven intelligences, learning byte, feelings about school/teachers, specific learning disabilities, possible labels, patterned learning, sensory, visual, and auditory integration processing, maturational age, giftedness, emotional/mental intelligence, possible food/beverage sensitivities, water preferences, toxic minerals, environmental pollutants, electro-magnetic stressors, etc.

At the Whole Child Institute, there are no invasive procedures. Our specialists know how to spot a problem and deal with it at the cause and core level. The action plan helps parents make educated choices, find appropriate resources and learning strategies; while helping their child overcome major obstacles. **Call: (651) 452-9281 or 1-877-296-8007, schedule one today!**

ORGANIZATIONS

Listing of Brain Gym Classes
Edu-Kineseology Foundation
P.O. Box 3396
Ventura, CA 93006
1-800-356-2109

Books and Resources
Practical Allergy
Research Foundation
Pres. Dr. Doris Rapp
PO Box 60
Buffalo, NY 14223-0060
1-800-787-8780

Physicians Referral
American Academy of
Environmental Medicine
10 East Randolph Street
New Hope, PA 18938
(215) 862-4544

Fast Forward
Auditory Integration Therapy
Scientific Learning
Corporation
1995 University Avenue
Suite 400
Berkeley, CA 94704
(510) 665-9700

International Listing for Visual
Integration Processing Programs
COVD
International Listing for
Certified Behavioral
Optometrists/Therapists
1-888-268-3770
http://www.optcom3.com/covd/
index.html

Brain Research
Brain Research Foundation
Chicago, IL
(312) 782-4311

Visual Integration Therapy
(Brochures/Equipment)
American Optometric Assoc.
243 N. Lindbergh Blvd.
St. Louis, MO 63141
(314) 991-4100

National Therapist Listing for
EZT—Ersdal Zone Therapy
Academy of Dynamic
Integrative Therapy
Director Christine Horvath
1-800-250-4974

Food Additive Sensitivities
Feingold Assoc. of the U.S.
(Nutrition's role in behavior,
learning and health problems)
P.O. Box 6550
Alexandria, VA 22306
(703) 768-3287

Nutrasweet, how bad is it?
Aspartame Consumer Safety
Network (toxic affects of sugar
substitutes) Books, Audios or
Videos—Clearing house for
research and resources
Aspartame Consumer Safety
Network, Founder:
Mary Stoddard
PO Box 780634
Dallas, TX 75378
1-800-969-6050
http://web2.airmail.net/marystod

Ringing in the ears
American Tinnitus Assoc.
P.O. Box 5
Portland, OR 97207
(Send SASE for information)
(503) 248-9985

Mental Health **(NIMH)**
Nat. Inst. of Mental Health
1-800-64-PANIC

ORGANIZATIONS

Depression
**National Depressive and
Manic-Depressive Association
730 N. Franklin St., Suite 501
Chicago, Illinois 60610-3526
1-800-826-3632**
www.ndmda.org

Awareness Through Movement
**Feldenkrais® Resources
830 Bancroft Way, Suite 112
Berkeley, CA 94710
1-800-765-1907**

Ideas for building Internal Assets
in youth. **Search Institute
700 S. Third St., Suite 210
Minneapolis, MN 55415
1-800-888-7828**

Curriculum for
Patterned Learners
**SRA/McGraw-Hill
220 E. Danieldale Road
DeSoto, TX 75115-2490
1-888/SRA-4Kids
(1-888-772-4543)**

Learning Disabilities
**L.D.A. National Office
4156 Library Road
Pittsburgh, PA 15234
(412) 341-1515**

Affordable alternative healthcare
provider network—no insurance.
Discounted cash program for
services such as Chiropractic,
Massage, Dentistry, Vision, etc.
**Adjusted America (Minnesota)
1260 Yankee Doodle Road
Suite 100
Eagan, MN 55121
(651) 454-0706**

Blood Sugar Imbalance
**National Association for
Alternative Medicine—The
National Diabetes Foundation
Division** Free Diabetes Resource
Guide. Call: **1-800-681-3552**

Impact of Media on Children
**National Institute on Media and
the Family** David Walsh, Ph.D.
**606 24th Ave. So., Suite 606
Minneapolis, MN 55454
(612) 672-5437
1-888-672-5437**

Personality Analysis through
facial features...
**International Institute of
Personology and the
Personology Institute—
Training Center
507 Capitola Avenue
Capitola, CA 95010-2759
(408) 476-1632**

Information of Allergies
**Allergy Research Group
400 Preda Street
P.O. Box 480
San Leandro, CA 94577
1-800-545-9960**

Manufactures and Distributor
Information see appendix in...
**Prescription for Nutritional
Healing, by James F. Balch,
M.D. & Phyllis Balch, C.N.C.
Avery Publishing Group
ISBN 0-89529-727-2**

Sleep Disorders
**American Sleep Disorders
1610 14th Street, Suite 300
Rochester, MN 55901
(507) 287-6006**

ORGANIZATIONS

Autism
Autism Research Institute
4182 Adams Avenue
San Diego, CA 92116
Founder: Bernard Rimland, Ph.D.
(619) 563-6840 Phone/Fax

Defeat Autism Now (DAN)
Cure Autism Now (CAN)
(both are foundations)
Dr. William Shaw Ph.D. is an
active member of both of these
organizations. Dr. Shaw wrote
Biological Treatments for Autism
and PDD—A comprehensive and
easy-to-read guide to the most
current research and medical
therapies for autism and PDD.
For more information contact
Dr. Shaw at (913) 341-8949 or
e-mail williamsha@aol.com

Autism and yeast
Dr. Bruce Semon M.D. Ph.D.
Contributing author for
Biological Treatments for
Austism and PDD. Dr. Semon
and his wife Lori Kornblum, are
in the process of publishing a
cookbook implementing a diet
free of yeast and fermented foods,
casein, gluten, eggs, corn, and
soy.
Dr. Semon can be reached at:
250 W. Coventry Court, St. 101
Glendale Wisconsin 53217,
(414) 352-6500

Facial ticks (twitches) etc.
Tourette Syndrome Association
42-40 Bell Blvd., Suite 205
Bayside, NY 11361-2820
1-800-237-0717

Anxiety
Anxiety Disorder Assoc. of
America
6000 Executive Blvd., Suite 200
Rockville, MD 20852-4004
(301) 231-9350

Neurologicl Awareness
American Chiropractic
Association
1701 Clarendon Blvd.
Arlington, VA 22209
(703) 276-8800

Nutritional Testing, etc.
Contact Reflex Analysis and
Nutritional Research
Foundation
International Provider Listing
www.CRAhealth.org
P.O. Box 914
Jenison, MI 49429-0914

Parker College
Nat. CRA(sm) Seminars List
1-800-266-GRAD

Sensory Integration Processing
Professional Development
Programs
14398 North 59th Street
Oak Park Heights, MN 55082
(651) 439-8865
e-mail: ProDevPrg@aol.com

Behavioral Styles
Adult/Teen Programs
Vistar Integrated Programs—
MN (International)
5560 Nathan Lane North, #1
Plymouth, MN 55442
1-888-923-5669
e-mail VISTARMN@aol.com

ORGANIZATIONS

Info. concerning health problems
related to common yeast
(Candida albicans)
**International Health
Foundation, Inc.**
Founder: William Crook, M.D.
**P.O. Box 3494
Jackson, TN 38303
Hotline: (901) 660-7090**

P.A.R. (Parents Against Ritalin)
**P.A.R. National Headquarters
225 South Brady
Claremore, OK 74017
1-800-469-5929**

Reading, Writing & Spelling
**The Riggs Institute (prod./sem.)
4185 S.W. 102nd Avenue
Beaverton, Oregon 97005
(503) 646-9459**

Non-Toxic Building Materials
**Shelter Supply™, Inc.
17725 Juniper Path
Lakeville, MN 55044-9482
1-800-762-8399**
http://www.shelter-mn.com
e-mail: shelter@bitstream.net

Book: Vegetarian Journal's
(magazine) Guide to Natural
Foods Restaurants in the U.S. and
Canada (1998) (Also food stores)
From the Vegetarian Resource
Group. Forward by
Lindsay Wagner
Avery Publishing Group, NY
ISBN 0-89529-837-6

ChADD
**Children and Adults with
Attention Deficit Disorder
1-800-233-4050**

Vaccines, making informed
choices: **National Vaccine
Information Center
512 W. Maple Ave. #206
Vienna, VA 22180
1-800-909-SHOT
Newsletter: Vaccine Reaction**

Self-Talk Tapes, etc.
**The Self-Talk Institute
Self-Talk Information Services
5930 E. Pima, Suite 144
Tucson, AZ 85712
1-800-982-8196**

Depression/Seasonal Affective
Disorder Products…
**Light Therapy Products
6125 Ives Lane N.
Plymouth, MN 55442
(612) 559-1613
Rental Program Available
http://home.sprynet.com/spry
net/1therapy**

Meter for electromagnetic
radiation, books, etc.
**N.E.E.D.S. (catalog)
National Ecological and
Environmental Delivery System
527 Charles Avenue 12A
Syracuse, NY 13209
1-800-634-1380**

**STRAND BOOKSTORE
8 miles of books: new, old, rare.
Two and a half million in stock.
Reviewers copies of new books/
paperbacks 50% off list price.
Free Catalogs!
828 Broadway (at 12th St.)
New York, NY 10003-4805
(212) 473-1452 E-mail:
strand@strandbooks.com**

Glossary of Terms

ABC Kid Label: Sarcastic description of a child who is dealing with many symptoms falling under many labels at one time. Example: ADD, ODD, OCD, and PDD.

Abstraction Disability: Difficulty understanding the difference between words when based in context such as, "the dog" versus "you dog." Misunderstanding of jokes and puns.

Aculculia: Inability to understand or use mathematical symbols or functions, yet reading and writing may not be a problem

Agnosia: Inability to recognize objects or events through the sense of sight, sound, and/ or touch. Example: Can not recognize an alarm or siren, and/or understand the spoken word, and/or recognize objects by touch.

Agrammatism (arammalogia): Inability to use words correctly in sentences.

Agraphia: Inability to write words, manipulate a writing instrument and/or master syntactic principles.

Alexia: Inability to read even though vision and intelligence is normal. Also called word blindness due to a dysfunction in the central nervous system.

Amphetamines: A group of drugs used to stimulate the cerebral cortex of the brain. Sometimes used to treat ADD/ADHD. Amphetamines are speed.

Amygdala: Located behind the ears, deep within the brain. May play a part in extinguishing an emotional memory. Acts as a storehouse for emotional memory.

Anarthia: Inability to say words correctly due to damage to the nervous system.

Anomia: Inability to recall the names of people, places, or objects.

Aphasia: Inability to express oneself through speech, writing, or signs, or to comprehend written or spoken language, yet may know what is wanted to be said.

Applied Kinesiology: Kinesiology is the study of muscular movement. In 1960 Dr. George Goodheart, an American chiropractor, began to expound on the underlying concepts of applied kinesiology. It is an ecclectic blend of biofeedback, Chinese accupressure, emotional stress release, neuro-lymphatic massage and maniputaltion of the bodies natural electrical flow.

Apraxia: Inability to draw shapes and figures or copy words and letters, produce and sequence the movements necessary for writing.

Asperger's Syndrome: A form of Pervasive Developmental Disorder with age appropriate skills other than social interaction. Significant impairment in social and occupational functioning. Great difficulty with change as well as transitioning from activity to activity. Sometimes referred to as High Functioning Autism.

Asymbolia: Inability to use or understand symbols associated with mathematics, science or music.

Attention Deficit Disorder (ADD): Attention Deficit Disorder without hyperactivity. Problems with concentration, difficulty following the rules, starting something new but never finishing, easily distracted, may seem depressed. Many reasons why, no one cause.

Attention Deficit Hyperactive Disorder (ADHD): Attention Deficit Disorder with hyperactivity. Difficulty sitting still, following directions and paying attention—easily distracted, incessant talking, interrupting others, trouble with listening, messy, loses things, impulsive, etc. Many reasons why, no one cause.

Auditory Association: Ability to relate to and understand concepts presented orally.

Auditory Blending: Blending of letter sounds in order to form a whole word.

Auditory Closure: Ability to understand a partially spoken word. Example: ele ant (elephant).

Auditory Discrimination: Ability to hear similarities and differences of sounds, such as p and b or words such as pail and bail.

Auditory Integration Processing: Not how one hears, but how one processes what one hears.

Auditory Memory: Ability to remember sounds, syllables, and words.

Auditory Perception: Ability to differentiate between similar sounds or pick out one specific sound from several other sounds.

Auditory Processing: Ability to use the ear and brain to make sense of what is heard.

Auditory Reception: Ability to derive meaning from orally presented material.

Auditory Sequential Memory: Ability to reproduce a sequence of auditory stimuli.

Autism: A developmental disability on a continuum from mild to severe with onset usually in the first three years of life. A behaviorally defined syndrome characterized by an uneven developmental profile and disturbances in interaction, communication, and perceptual organization.

Bach Flower Remedies: Thirty-eight homeopathically prepared flower essences, discovered by Edward Bach. These essences are directed toward healing the personality, mood, and emotional outlook of an individual. Dr. Bach believed if a patients emotional balance was corrected the bodies natural ability to thwart illness would be strengthened.

Behavior Modification: A system of changing negative behavior without regard to the causes of that behavior.

Bilateral: Both sides of the body working together.

Binocular Fusion: Blending of separate images from each eye into one, meaningful image.

Bio-feedback: Feedback of what the body does autonomically without concious awareness. EEG Bio-feedback (electro-encelphalogram) is a training process much like learning a sport. Helps a person develop focused attention and/or relaxation while attending.

Bipolar Disorder: A mood disorder with emotional highs (manic) and lows (depression). Can involve rapid shifts between manic moods and anger or depression.

Body Image: Awareness of where ones body is in space. Example: Lying on a bed or sitting in a chair.

Brushing Technique: Received its slang name from the Willbarger Approach which uses a surgical brush to stimulate tactile receptors on the body. This technique does not actually involve brushing. Pressure of the stroke, which must be firm enough to bend the bristles, best describes this technique.

Candida Albicans: Common yeasts within the body. Like many other tiny organisms, candida puts out toxins or poisons, which weaken the immune system and irritate the nervous system. Candida overgrowth also disturbs the mucous membrane of the gut. Allergens penetrate these membranes and go to other parts of the body. Anitbiotics encourage the growth of the common yeast, Candida albicans cause headaches, hyperactivity, brain fog, irritability, inattention, etc.

Cerebral Cortex: Outer layer of the cerebrum (gray matter). The cerebral cortex controls thinking, feeling, and voluntary movement.

Cerebral Hemispheric Dominance: Term used to point out that right, left or balanced dominance has been established.

Cerebrum: Main part of the brain which forms the largest part of the central nervous system.

Children and Adults with Attention Deficit Disorder (ChADD)
Organization: local and national. (see Appendix I—Organizations.)

Cognitive: Pertaining to ideas or thoughts.

Colonics: Irrigation, using water, of toxins lining the colon. Similar to an enema but far more reaching, water flows through all five feet of the intestinal track.

Conceptualization: Process of forming a general idea from what is observed. Example: Inferring that apples, bananas, and oranges are fruit.

Conduct Disorder: Persistent antisocial behavior (theft, cheating at games, lying, etc.) Conduct disorders often co-occur with depression, low self image, problem solving skills, learning disorders, substance abuse, or ADHD.

Criterion-Referenced Test: A test which has a standard measure of performance.

Cross Dominance: Also called mixed dominance. Example: An individual may be right footed and right eyed, but left-handed.

Decoding: Process of getting meaning from written or spoken symbols.

Depression: A mood disorder occurring with or without manic episodes of bipolar disorder. Sad, over tired, or expressing hopelessness. Some people become angry or irritable, abuse drugs or alcohol, get in trouble.

Detoxification: Removal of toxins from the body.

Dietary Supplement: Vitamins, minerals, amino-acids, etc. which supplement what a person can't get from their diet.

Diffuser: A small electrical machine used to disperse an essential oil into the air.

Directional Problem: Inability in distinguishing right from left, up from down, forward from backward. Difficulty knowing where ones body is in space.

Distilled Water: Distillation involving boiling of water and then condensing and collecting the steam. If done correctly distilled water is usually very high quality.

Distractibility: Shifting of attention from a task to a sound, or other stimuli that normally occurs in the environment.

Dominance: Preference when using a hand, foot, ear, or eye.

Due Process: Parents have the right to request a full review of the educational program developed for their child. A due process hearing may be requested to ensure that all requirements of P.L. (Public Law) 101-456 have been met.

Dysgraphia: Difficulty with the ability to produce legible writing.

Dyslexia: Impairment in the ability to read. May be due to a learning disability or other factors. Person who sees words upside down, reversed, blurred or backwards. Sometimes used to denote inability to read.

Early Childhood Special Education (ECSE): Check for local programs in your community. Government/Community sponsored program.

Educational Behavior Disorder (EBD): This is not a medical label, but a school label and is a category of special education. Denotes students with behavioral and/or emotional problems that affect their ability to learn.

Educational Diagnostic Test: A test designed to identify weaknesses and strengths in reading, mathematics or other subjects. Results used in planning how and what to teach.

Electromagnetic Radiation (EMR): Radiation from power lines, video display terminals, micro-waves, televisions, pagers, and other sources.

Emotionally Disturbed: Diminished ability to learn and to cope with ones environment.

Encoding: Process of changing oral language into written symbols.

Essential Oils: Oils of various scents and medicinal properties derived from the life force of plants.

Expressive Language: Communication through writing, speaking, and/or gestures.

Eye-hand Coordination: Ability of the eyes and hands to work together to complete a task, such as drawing writing, walking, or running.

Eye Tracking: Ability of the eyes to follow an object.

Feedback: Information received from the body's activities, which tells an individual how he or she is performing.

Figure-Ground Discrimination (perception): Ability to sort out important information from ones environment. Example: Hearing and processing the teachers voice while ignoring the classroom noises or being able to see and process a picture of a bear even though it is blending in with the scenery. Figure—as in object. Ground—as in background.

Fine Motor: Use of small muscles for such tasks as writing, tying shoes, zipping a jacket, etc. For this type of task precision is more important than strength.

Food Sensitivities: Allergies create physical signs, whereas food sensitivities affect a persons emotional well-being and physical health.

Gross Motor: Use of large muscles for activities requiring strength and balance. Example: walking, running, and jumping.

High Functioning Autism: Mild symptoms of Pervasive Developmental Disorder, characterized by social impairments. This term is used interchangeably with Aspergers Syndrome.

Hippocampus: Located somewhat above the amygdala (see amygdala in glossary) deep within the brain. Remembers the factual information while the amygdala remembers the emotional overtone.

Hyperactivity (hypokinesis): Disorganized and disruptive behavior characterized by constant and excessive movement.

Hypertonia: Muscles being too tight restricting coordinated movement.

Impusivity: Reacting to a situation without considering the consequences.

Independent Learning: Ability to teach oneself. This ability comes from a strong foundation in the basic skills of learning.

Individualized Education Program (I.E.P.): A written plan for educating a child with special education status. The purpose of the IEP is to implement the law called the Individuals with Disabilities Act (IDEA), often referred to as Public Law 101-456.

Input Disabilities: Inability to correctly process, either visually or auditorally, information being seen or heard.

Invasive Procedures: Tending to invade healthy tissue. Example: using a needle for a blood test.

Kinesthesis: Body movements and the ability of the body to be aware of these movements.

Kumon: A system of learning developed over forty years ago by Mr. Toru Kumon of Osaka, Japan in order to help his son Takashi who was not doing well with school textbooks. Takashi was most likely a patterned learner. Because of the math worksheets his father designed, he was doing integral calculus by sixth grade. Their neighbors asked for the worksheets and eventually Mr. Kumon set up franchises all over the world. Today students study math and reading, as well as different languages.

L.R.E.: Least Restrictive Environment. P.L. (Public Law) 101-456 uses L.R.E. when it states that children with disabilities are educated with children without disabilites to the maximum extent possible and that the placement of a child with a disability outside the regular classroom occurs only when the nature or severity of the disability is such that education in a regular class with the use of supplementary aides and services cannot be achieved satisfactorily.

Laterality: Tendency to use the hand, foot, eye and ear on a particular side of the body.

Learning Byte: The human byte or learning byte correlates with how much information a person can retain in a twenty-four hour period. For most people this byte is between two and seven. If ones learning byte for numbers is three, and four numbers are taught today, all four numbers will be forgotten by tomorrow. The extra piece of information that went over the byte actually blows a "fuse" in the brain and all of the new information is lost.

Learning Disorder: Damage or impairment to the nervous system, causing a learning disabililty.

Learning Style: How someone learns and processes information.

Left Brain Hemisphere: Refers to the left side of the brain which generally houses logic, sequential thinking, abstract thinking, ability to write, read, learn phonics, talk, recite, follow directions, listen, etc..

Left-Right Discrimination: Understanding the difference between using the left side of the body vs. the right side of the body.

Limbic System: Sometimes referred to as the emotional brain.

Mainstream: A special needs student who is mainstreamed is a student who is spending most of his class time in a classroom of a variety of students on various levels, including high achievers.

Maturational Age: Unlike a persons chronological age (age since birth,) the maturational age of a person is the age the person functions at mentally and emotionally.

Medical Model: Crisis intervention model—looks for symptoms and address the symptoms. Doctors in the medical model are trained to treat crisis and have little, if any, training in nutrition and how it affects the body physically as well as emotionally.

Midline: Imaginary line dividing the body in half from the top of the head to the feet. We are not born with the ability to cross midline. Some children need exercises in order to develop this ability.

Modality: Sensory channel used to acquire information, visual, auditory, and tactile, kinestetic, olfactory (odors) and gustatory (taste) are the most common modalities.

Multi-Disciplinary Team: A child support group which includes, the student's classroom teacher, student being evaluated for special education services, his or her parents, principal, and several educational specialists. The group assesses the student and if the student qualifies for special education services, writes an individualized education program (I.E.P.) for the student, and continues meeting together to ensure the I.E.P. is being followed.

Multi-Sensory Learning: Learning in ways that combine seeing, hearing, saying and doing.

Neurological Examination: Examination of the nervous system.

Neurotoxins: Toxins which have an ill affect on the nervous system.

Non-Gluten Grains: Gluten is a protein found in wheat, oats, rye, barley, spelt and buckwheat. Non-gluten grains include amaranth, brown rice, coarse cornmeal, millet, quinoa, and wild rice. Gluten-free flours include arrowroot, amaranth, brown rice, garbanzo (chick pea), soybean, potato, nut and seed, and legume. Gluten-free pasta includes corn, quinoa, rice, amaranth, and soy. Digestive problems can be associated with an intolerance to gluten.

Nutritionally Oriented: Understanding of how nutrition affects the body, especially the brain, nervous system, and emotions.

Occupational Therapy (O.T.): A form of therapy which looks at the whole person. People dealing with developmental problems, the aging process, social, psychological, or learning difficulties can benefit from this therapy. The goal of O.T. is to assist each individual in achieving an independent productive and satisfying life.

Obsessive Cumpulsive Disorder (OCD): Persistent disturbing preoccupation with an idea, feeling, cleanliness, objects, etc.

Oppositional Defiant Disorder (ODD): A disorder which involves opposing what one is being told or asked to do. Non-compliant behavior.

OrthoMolecular Approach: Treatment of disease by increasing, decreasing, or otherwise controlling the intake of natural substances especially vitamins.

Orton-Gillingham Approach: A method for teaching individuals with learning disabilities. The technique, devised by Dr. Samuel T. Orton, of the Orton Dyslexia Society, Anna Gillingham, and Bessie Stillman, stresses a multi-sensory approach to learning.

Output Disabilities: Language, difficulty expressing oneself using words. Motor, difficulty expressing oneself using writing, drawing, or gesturing.

P.A.R.: Parents Against Ritalin: Organization—see Appendix I—Organizations

Perceptual Motor: Muscle activity resulting from information received through the senses.

Periodic Review: Three year review of a students IEP (Individual Education Plan)

Perservation: Repeating of words, motions, or tasks. A child who perseverates often has difficulty shifting to a new task and continues the old task long after others (peers, etc.) have stopped.

Personology: A fifty year old science that involves the study of human beings through their physical structure.

Pervasive Development Disorder (PDD): A group of conditions (Autism, Rett's Disorder, Childhood Disintegrative Disorder, Asperger's Disorder) marked by distortions, deviations, and delays in social and motor skills, language, attention, perception, and reality testing.

Phonics or Phonetics: Letter sounds and letter combinations known as phonograms or chunks, which have a specific sound or sounds.

Physiological: Characteristics of a physical nature during normal functioning.

Preventive Medical Model: <u>Looks for</u> the <u>cause</u> of symptoms and <u>addresses</u> the <u>cause</u> <u>with natural methods of intervention.</u>

Reversal Frequency: Confusing letters (b/d , p/q) and/or words (saw/ was,) (pots/spots)..

Reverse-Osmosis: A water purification system that has the ability to squeeze out small particles which pollute water. A process where water is forced through a very thin membrane to remove dissolved toxic as well as non-toxic minerals

Right Brain Hemisphere: The side of the brain that usually houses holistic thinking, ability to visualize, intuition, fantasy, feelings and emotions, singing, music, art expression, color sensitivity, mathematical computation, spatial relationships, etc.

Section 504 Plan: Advocacy tool for parents of children with disabilities. Section 504 of the 1973 Rehabilitation Act is a civil rights act for students dealing with learning and/or behavior challenges and is not to be confused with the special education process. This is a federal law that governs students who are not picked up by special education services yet need to have accommodations in their school curriculum and/or setting.

Self-concept: Ones overall opinion of oneself.

Self-Talk: An internal voice that gives us affirmations (both positive and negative). Self-talk often needs to be taught to special needs students as a way to walk themselves through difficult math problems or while learning a new skill.

Sensory Integration Processing: Processing of information taken in through the sense of touch, taste, sight, etc.

Sequencing Disability: Inability to put a logical sequence together. Ex.: Putting separate pictures in the correct order for the correct sequence in time—wheat in the field, a bag of flour, a clump of dough, an oven, a loaf of bread.

Spatial Awareness: Being aware of where ones body is in space.

Spatial Relationships: The relationship of objects to each other or oneself to an object.

Specific Language Disability (SLD): A specific disorder involving speech and language.

Spectrum Disorder: An array of the components arranged in the order of some varying characteristics. Autism is a spectrum disorder.

Standardized Test: See criterion-referenced test.

Steam Distilled Water: Steam virtually removes all micro-organisms and impurities leaving behind dissolved solids, salts, heavy metals, etc. Carbon filtration can be added to assure purity.

Support System: A group of people who are willing and able to support ones efforts of reality.

Tactile: Relating to the sense of touch.

Validity: The extent to which a test measures what it claims to measure.

Vestibular System: Most primitive system, beginning its development well before birth. This system interprets and responds to the position of the head in relation to gravity and movement. Individuals with a vestibular system that is functioning poorly may feel dizzy, lose their balance easily, have poor coordination, low muscle tone, and/or poor eye contact.

Vestibular Activities: Include rocking, swinging, jumping on a trampoline, or any gross motor activity involving movement of the head.

Vibratory Frequency: A reading of electrical vibration in the body, food, or other living things.

Visual Acuity: The keenness of vision, ability to see.

Visual Closure: Ability to close off in ones mind an incomplete picture or letter and determine what it is.

Visual Discrimination: Ability to determine differences of shapes, colors sizes, positions and distances.

Visual Fixation: Ability to perform a visual task without losing sight of words or an object. Example: Poor visual fixation might mean losing ones place while reading.

Visual Integration Processing: Not how we see, but how we process what we see. The ability to visualize, understand, and apply the information that comes through the eyes.

Visual Memory: Ability to remember what is seen.

Visualization: Ability to hold a picture in the mind and move it around. Visualization is needed for carry-overs and borrowing in math and for good reading comprehension.

Whole Food: Food that is closest to its natural state. Whole food has maximum nutritive value.

Word Attack Skills: Skills which help break down words so they can be read. See encoding and decoding.

Nutrition Book List

STEP BY STEP APPROACH TO NUTRITIONAL HEALING: For those seeking optimum health for the body, mind, and spirit, by Leanne Woodland & Lynn McDonough
Abundant Living, Inc.
1-888-548-4680   E-mail:
book@abundantlivinginc.com

FOOD ADDITIVES
A Shopper's Guide To What's Safe & What's Not
by Christine Hoza Farlow, D.C.
Escondido, CA 92026-1488
(619) 735-8108
ISBN 0-9635635-0-5

BE YOUR OWN DOCTOR
A Positive Guide to Natural Living
by Ann Wigmore
Avery Publishing Group
ISBN 0-89529-193-2

VITAMIN AND MINERAL DECODER
with Dr. Kate Short
Dynamo House, Melbourne, Austrailia
ISBN 0-949266-32-9

HOME SAFE HOME
by Debra L. Dadd
Putnam
ISBN 0-8747-785-9-X

LOUISE TENNEY'S NUTRIONAL GUIDE
With Food Combining
by Louise Tenney
Woodland Books
Provo, Utah
ISBN 0-913923-79-6

THE FOOD SENSITIVITY DIET
Based on the Remarkable Scientific Breakthrough in Cytotoxic Nutrition
by Doug A. Kaufmann Freundlich Books
New York
ISBN 0-88191-003-1

ALLERGY & CANDIDA COOKING—ROTATIONAL STYLE, by Sandra K. Lewis
Canary Connect Publications
P.O. Box 5317
Coralville, Iowa 52241-0317
(319) 351-2317

PRESCRIPTION FOR NUTRITIONAL HEALING Second Edition, A practical A-Z Reference...Drug-Free
by James Balch, M.D.
Avery Publishing
ISBN 0-89529-727-2

THE YEAST CONNECTION HANDBOOK
This Easy-to-Follow Guide Brings Readers the Latest Information about Yeast-Related Disorders and How to Overcome Them
by William G. Crook, M.D.
Professional Books
Jackson, Tennessee 38301
ISBN 0-933478-23-2

VITACHART
A Guide to Vitamins and Minerals
by Carolyn Heller West
Bronx, New York 10463
(718) 796-7413

DIET FOR A NEW AMERICA—Video
How Your Food Choices Affect Your Health, Happiness and the Future of Life on Earth
by John Robbins
To order call 1-800-847-4014

LICK THE SUGAR HABIT
Sugar Addiction Upsets Your Whole Body Chemistry—Highly Recom. by Lendon Smith
by Nancy Appleton, Ph.D.
Avery Publishing Group, Inc.
ISBN 0-89529-386-2

WHY SHOULD I EAT BETTER?
Simple Answers to All your Nutritional Questions
by Linda Messinger
ISBN 0-89529-508-3

FOOD CHEMICAL SENSITIVITY
Discover New Diets Eliminating:
Salicytes,Tartrazine, Metabisulphite, Benzoic Acid, MSG, Yeasts, Toxic Metals
by Robert Buist, Ph.D.
ISBN 0-89529-399-4

SEVEN WEEKS TO SOBRIETY
The Proven Program to Fight Alcoholism Through Nutrition
by Joan Mathews Larson, Ph.D.
Fawcett Columbine Books
ISBN 0-449-90896-8

IS THIS YOUR CHILD?
by Doris Rapp
William Morrow & Co.
ISBN 0-688-119-077

HIDDEN FOOD ALLERGIES
How to Discover if You Have Food Allergies & What to do to Sucessfully Overcome Them
by Stephen Astor, M.D.
Avery Publishing Group
Garden City Park, New York
ISBN 0-89529-369-2

Books by Mark Percival
INFANT NUTRITION
Your Child's Foundation for Health
FUNCTIONAL DIETETICS
The Core of Health Integration
TEAMING UP FOR A HEALTHIER YOU
Understanding Healthcare & Stress Management
Health Coach Systems International Inc.
3 Waterloo St.
New Hamberg, Ont.
Canada N0B 2g0
(519) 662-2520

DEPRESSION AND NATURAL MEDICINE
A Nutrition Approach To Depression and Moos Swings
by Rita Elkins
Woodland
ISBN 1-885670-01-X

A HEALTHY HEAD START
A Worry -Free Guide to Feeding Young Children
by Mary Abbott Hess, M.S., R.D.
Henry Holt and Company
New York, New York 10011
ISBN 0-8050-1329-6

PYCNOGENOL
The Super "Protector" Nutrient
by Richard A. Passwater, Ph.D. &
Chithan Kandaswami, Ph.D.
Keats Publishing
27 Pine Street, Box 876
New Canaan, Connecticut
06840-0876
ISBN 0-87983-648-2

COLLOIDAL SILVER
The Natural Antibiotic
Alternative
(kills bacteria & virus on contact)
by Zane Baranowski, CN
Healing Wisdom Publications
New York, New York 10023
ISBN 0-9647080-1-9

**WHAT ARE WE FEEDING
OUR KIDS?**
What Parents Must Know about
their Children's Unhealthful Diets
by Michael F. Jacobson, Ph.D.
Workman Publishing Group 708
Broadway
New York, NewYork 10003
ISBN 1-781563-051012

**THE GREAT PYCNOGENOL
FACT BOOK**
With Information on other Health
Enhancing Products
by Eugene Lewis
Marketing Research International
P.O. Box 49711
Blaine, Minnesota 55449-0711
1-800-226-6557

**THE FOUR PILLARS OF
HEALING**
by Leo Galland, M.D.
Random House
ISBN 0-679-44888-8

**DR. CROOK DISCUSSES
YEASTS**
And How They Can Make You
Sick, by William G. Crook, M.D.
Professional Books
P.O. Box 3246
Jackson, Tennessee 38303
(901) 423-5400
ISBN 0-933478-07-0

THE GARDEN WITHIN
Acidophilus-Candida Connection
by Keith W. Sehnert, M.D.
World Health, Inc.
1477Rollins Road
Burlingame, California 94010
ISBN 0-9624780-0-8

WHY CAN'T I EAT THAT?
Helping Kids Obey Medical Diets
by John F. Taylor
R. & E. Publications
P.O. Box 2008
Saratoga, California 95070
(408) 866-6303
ISBN 0-88247-981-4

NUTRITION ADVISOR
Prevention Magazine's Ultimate
Guide to the Health-Boosting &
Health-Harming Factors in Your
Diet
by Mark Bricklin
Rodale Press
ISBN 0-87596-225

EAT SMART THINK SMART
How to Use Nurtients and
Supplments to Achieve
Maximum Mental and Physical
Performance
by Robert Haas
Harper Collins Publishers
ISBN 0-06-017044-1

**NATURAL IMMUNITY
INSIGHT ON DIET AND
AIDS**
Discover happiness in making a
recovery through the natural
methods described
in this book
by Noboru B. Muramot
ISBN 0-918860-48-2

**DEPRESSION CURED AT
LAST**—Act on her advise and
you'll fell great, by Dr. Sherry A.
Rogers, SK Publishing, PO Box
40101,Sarasota, Florida 34242
ISBN 1-887202-00-5

THE ADD AND ADHD DIET
Contributing factors and natural
treatments for symptoms of ADD
and Hyperactivity
by Rachel Bell
ISBN 1-884820-29-8

**A.D.D. THE NATURAL
APPROACH**
Natural therapies support the
body's innate ability to heal itself,
by Nina Anderson & Howard
Peiper
ISBN 9-781884-820199

**HOW TO REACH AND
TEACH ADD/ADHD
CHILDREN**
by Sandra F. Rief
Center for Applied Research
ISBN 087-628-413-6

CHEMICAL SENSITIVITY
Environmental diseases and
pollutants-how they hurt us, how
to deal with them
by Sherry A. Rogers M.D.
A Keats Good Health Guide

DIGESTIVE ENZYMES
Digest and absorb or your body is
actually suffering from
malnutrition and enjoy less than
optimal health.
by Jeffery Bland Ph.D.
Keates Publishing
ISBN 0-87983-331-9

COLON HEALTH
The key to a Vibrant Life! You
can regain the vitality of your
youth
by Dr. Norman W. Walker
Norman Press
ISBN 9-89019-069-0

**YOUR BODY'S MANY CRIES
FOR WATER** (2nd Ed.)
You are not sick, you are thirsty!
by F. Batmanghelidj, M.D.
Global Health Solutions
ISBN 0-9629942-3-5

**EASING ANXIETY &
STRESS NATURALLY**
A natural, drugless program to
ease stress, nervous tension and
emotional disturbance
by Susan M. Mark M.D.
A Keats Good Health Guide
Keats Publishing
ISBN 0-87983-728-4

BEYOND ADD/ADHD
An effective Holistic, mind-body
approach
Hunting for Reasons in the Past &
Present
by Rita Debroitner & Avery Hart
Underwood Book, Inc.
ISBN 0-8092-3076-3

**STOPPPING
HYPERACTIVITY:
A NEW SOLUTION**
Symetric Tonic Neck Reflex,
complete exercise program
by Nancy O'Dell & Partriaia
Cook
Avery Publishing Group
ISBN 0-89529-789-2

**RAISING YOUR CHILD
TOXIC FREE**
by Needleman
Farrar Straus Giroux
ISBN 0-3742-4643-2

**WHAT ARE WE FEEDING
OUR KIDS?**
by M. Jacobson Ph.D.
Workman Publishing Co.
ISBN 156-305-101-X

KITCHEN FUN FOR KIDS
by Michael Jacobson
 Henry Holt & Co.
ISBN 080-504-503-1

**AMERICAN HEART
ASSOCIATION'S
KIDS COOKBOOK**
All recipes made by Real Kids in
Real Kitchens
Random House Publishers
ISBN 081-291-9300

AROMATHERAPY
The Essential Beginning
by D. Gary Young, N.D.
Essential Press Publishers
P.O. Box 9282
Salt Lake City, UT 84109
ISBN 0-9648187-0-1

**THE SAFE SHOPPER'S
BIBLE**
A consumer's guide to non-toxic
household products, cosmetics
and food **(great resource list)**
by David Steinman & Samuel S.
Epstein, M.D.
Macmillian
ISBN 0-02-082085-2

FOOD AND HEALING
How what you eat determines
your health, your well-being, and
the quality of your life
by Annemarie Colbin
Ballantine Books
ISBN 0-345-30385-7

**DIET FOR A POISONED
PLANET**
How to choose safe foods for you
and your family
by David Steinman
Ballantine Books
ISBN 0-345-37465-7

SUGAR BLUES
by William Duffy
Warner Books, Inc.
ISBN 0-446-34312-9

EAT RIGHT 4 YOUR TYPE
The individualized diet solution
by Dr. Peter J. D'Adamo
G. P. Putnam & Sons
ISBN 0-399-142255-X

**DEADLY DECEPTION—
STORY OF ASPARTAME**
(Toxicology Source Book)
by Mary Nash Stoddard
Odenwald Press
ISBN 1-884363-14-8
1-800-969-6050

THE FOOD ALLERGY BOOK
The foods that cause you pain and
discomfort, and how to take them
out of your diet
by William Walsh, M.D.
F.A.C.A. A.C.A. Publications
ISBN 0-9631544-7-8

**THE PARENT'S GUIDE
TO REFLEXOLOGY**
Helping your child overcome
illness and injury through touch
by Kevin & Barbara Kunz
Three Rivers Press
ISBN 0-517-88845-9

**EASY BREAD MAKING FOR
SPECIAL DIETS**
Use your bread machine, food
processor, or mixer to make:
Wheat-free, milk-free, lactose-
free, egg-free, gluten-free, yeast-
free, sugar-free, low fat, high
fiber, low fiber, low sodium,
diabetic and low calorie.
by Nicolette M. Dumke
Allergy Adapt, Inc.
ISBN 1-887-624-023

**SPECIAL DIETS FOR
SPECIAL KIDS:** Understanding
and Implementing Dietary
Intervention for Autistic Children,
Pub. Future Horizons
by Lisa Lewis Ph.D.
ISBN 1-885-47744-9

**THE FOUR PILLARS OF
HEALING**
by Leo Galland, M.D.
Random House, NY
ISBN 0-679-44888-8

**THE CURE FOR ALL
DISEASES—With Many Case
Studies,** by Hulda R. Clark,
Ph.D., N.D.
New Century Press
ISBN 1-890035-01-7

MAIL ORDER FOR HEALTHY FOODS

CELESTIAL HARVEST
2888 Bluff Street, Suite 114
Boulder, CO 80301
(303) 440-1972
FAX (303) 440-1004

WALNUT ACRES ORGANIC FARMS®
Whole Foods for Healthy
Living—direct from America's
Original Organic Farm
Catalog of organic foods
1-800-433-3998
hhtp://walnutacres.com

FOR HEALTH FOOD STORES OR WHOLE FOOD STORES IN YOUR AREA
Look in your Yellow Pages

VEGETARIAN JOURNAL'S GUIDE TO NATURAL FOODS RESTAURANTS IN THE UNITED STATES & CANADA
From the Vegetarian Resource Group,
Forward by Lindsay Wagner
(Listing of health food stores)
Avery Publishing Group, NY
ISBN 0-89529-654-3

EDUCATION BOOK LIST

THE DIFFICULT CHILD
by Stanley K Turecki & Leslie
Tonner, Bantam Books, Inc.
ISBN 0-553-34446-3

THE MANIPULATIVE CHILD
by Ernest W. Swihort
Macmillan Publishing Co.
ISBN 0-02-615700-4

THE OPTOMISTIC CHILD
A proven program to safegard
children against depression and
build lifelong resilience
by M. Siligman
Houghton-Mifflin
ISBN 0-06-097709-4

RAISING SELF-RELIANT
CHILDREN IN A SELF-
INDULGENT WORLD
Developing capable young people
by H.S. Glenn & Jane Nelsen
Prima Trade-Random House
ISBN 091-462-9921

SURRENDERING TO
MOTHERHOOD
Loosing your mind, finding your
soul by Iris Krasnow
Little Brown & Co.
ISBN 0-7868-6217-3

SIMPLIFY YOUR LIFE WITH
KIDS: 100 Ways to Make Family
Life Easier & More Fun
by Elaine St. James
Andrews McMael
ISBN 0-8362-3595-9

UNDERSTANDING YOUR
CHILD FROM BIRTH TO
SIXTEEN, by David Elkind
Allyn & Bacon, Inc.
ISBN 0-205-15971-0

THE ESSENCE OF
PARENTING
Becoming the parent you want to
be: loving, spontaneous,
confident , patient, relaxed, etc.
by Anne Johnson
Crossroad
ISBN 0-8245-1507-2

THE BOOK OF VIRTUES
A treasury of great moral stories
by William J. Bennett
Simon & Schuster
ISBN 0-671-68306-3

TEACHING YOUR CHILDREN
VALUES
by Linda & Richard Eyre
Fireside Publishers
Simon & Schuster
ISBN 0-671-76966-9

VALUES AND VIRTUES
    —Struggle Series—
*KIDS HAVE FEELINGS, TOO
    ISBN 156-476-0723
    ISBN 086-653-9271
*SOMETIMES I FEEL AWFUL
*HELPING CHILDREN
    UNDERSTAND DIVORCE
    ISBN 0866-53-8585
    (storybooks for kids grades 1-4)
    Chariot Victor Publishing

THE EMOTIONAL PROBLEMS
OF NORMAL CHILDREN
How Parents Can Understand &
Help, by S. Turecki M.D.
Bantam Trade
ISBN 055-307-4962

PARENTING WITH C.A.R.E.
Credibility, Assertiveness,
Responsibility,
Esteem Building
by Ray Nordine
Family Plus Press
P.O. Box 214
Dayton, MN 55327
(612) 920-0708

6 POINT PLAN FOR
RAINSING HAPPY, HEALTHY
CHILDREN, by J. Rosemond
Andrews McMeel
ISBN 0836228065

THE 7 HABITS OF HIGHLY
EFFECTIVE PEOPLE
by S. Covey
Simon & Schuster
ISBN 067-17086-35

7 HABITS OF HIGHLY
EFFECTIVE FAMILIES
Offers precious lessons in
creating and sustaining a strong
family culture in a turbulent
world, by Steven R. Covey
Franklin Covey Co.
ISBN 0-307-4408-7

STOP STRUGGLING WITH
YOUR CHILD
by Weinhaus & Friedman
Harper Collins
ISBN 006-09-64-812

HOW TO HAVE
INTELLIGENT & CREATIVE
CONVERSATIONS WITH
YOUR KIDS, by J. Healy
Double Day Paper
ISBN 038-547-2668

WHAT PRETEENS WANT
THEIR PARENTS TO KNOW
by Ryan Holladay
National Book Network
ISBN 156-977-4757
NO MORE NAGGING, NIT-
PICKING OR NUDGING
A Guide to Motivating, Inspiring,
and Influencing Kids Ages 10-18,
by Jim Wiltens
Deer Crossing Press
ISBN 0-345-34856-7

KIDS ARE WORTH IT!
Giving Your Child the Gift of
Inner Discipline
by Barbara Coloroso
William Morrow
ISBN 0-688-11622-1
1-800-729-1588

POSITIVE DISCIPLINE
A warm, practical, step-by-step
sourcebook for parents and
teachers. Kindness, respect,
encouragement—these are the
ingredients of positive discipline
by Jane Nelson, Ed. D.
Ballantine Books, NY
ISBN 0-345-34856-7

THE EXPLOSIVE CHILD
by Ross W. Greene, Ph.D.
Harper Collins
ISBN 0-06-017534-6
STEP: Systematic Training for
Effective Parenting
Early Childhoold STEP
STEP/Teen
Authors: Don Dinkmeyer, Sr. &
Gary D. McKay
1-800-328-2560

EXTRA ORDINARY KIDS
Nurturing and Championing your
child with special needs
by Cheri Fuller
Focus on the Family Publishers
ISBN 1-56179-558-5

ALL KIDS ARE OUR KIDS
What communities must do to
raise caring and responsible
children and adolescents
by Peter L. Benson
Jossey-Bass, Inc.
ISBN 0-787-910-686

EVERY CHILD AN ACHEIVER
A Parents Guide to the Kumon
Method. Kumon emphasizes
individual ability and the child's
ability to progress
by David W. Russell
INTERCULTURAL GROUP
1-800-ABC Math
ISBN 1-881267-09-1

BRINGING OUT THE
GIFTEDNESS IN YOUR CHILD
by Rita & Ken Dunn
John Wiley & Sons
ISBN 0-471-5280-3-X

PARENT'S GUIDE TO
RAISING A GIFTED CHILD
Recognizing and Developing
Your Child's Potential
by James Alvino and the editors
of Gifted Child Monthly
Ballantine Books
ISBN 0-345-33524-4

TEACHING WITH THE MIND
By Eric Jensen
ASCD, Alexandria, VA
1-800-933-2723
ISBN 0-87120-299-9

POSITIVE INVOLVEMENT
How to teach your child
habits for school success.
by Jack & Martha Youngblood
Brownwood Press
ISBN 0-9647295-0-4

BRAIN-BASED LEARNING
by Eric Jensen
The Brain Store, Inc.
ISBN 098-3783211

UNICORNS ARE REAL: A
RIGHT-BRAINED APPROACH
TO LEARNING
by Barbara Meister
Jalmar Press
ISBN 0-915-190-354

THE LEARNING
REVOLUTION
A life-long program for the
world's finest computer: your
amazing brain!, by Gordon
Dryden & Jeannette Vos, Ed.
Jalmar Press, CA
ISBN 1-880396-34-3

FIRST FUNDAMENTALS
Essential building blocks to raise
a brighter, happier child!
by Gordon Dryden & Colin Rose
Accelerated Learning
ISBN 0-905553-46-2

THE LEARNING BRAIN
How does our brain learn and
what you can do about it?
by Eric Jensen
Brain Store
ISBN 0-9637832-2-X

THE MIND MAP BOOK—
RADIANT THINKING
by Tony Buzan
NAL Dutton
ISBN 0-452-273-226

THE AMAZING BRAIN
by Robert Ornstein
Houghton Mifflin
ISBN 0-395-354-86-2

YOUR CHILD'S GROWING
MIND
A practical guide to Brain
Development & Learning from
Birth to Adolescence
by J. Healy
Double Day Paper
ISBN 038-54-69-306

SALT
Society for Accelerative Learning
and Teaching
Learning Forum
1725 South Coast Hwy.
Oceanside, CA 92054-5319
Organizes annual SALT
convention in the U.S.A.
(760) 722-0072

ACCELERATED LEARNING
by Colin Rose, Dell Publishing
ISBN 0-440-500-443

SLOW AND STEADY GET ME
READY—260 Weekly
Developmental Activities from
Birth to Age 5
by June R. Oberlander
Bio-Alpha, Inc.
ISBN 0-9622322-0-3

ALL KINDS OF MINDS
by Dr. Mel Levine
Educators Publishing
ISBN 0838820905

FRAMES OF MIND
THE UNSCHOOLED MIND
by Howard Gardner, Ph.D.
Basic Books/Harper Collins
ISBN 0-465-02510-2

BRAIN GYM: SIMPLE
ACTIVITIES FOR WHOLE
BRAIN LEARNING
by Paul & Gail Dennison
Edu-Kinesthetics, Inc.
P.O. Box 3396, Ventura, CA
93006-3396
(805) 650-3303
1-888-388-9898

TEACHING FOR THE TWO-
SIDED MIND
A guide to right brain/left brain
education
by Linda Verlee Williams
A Touchstone Book/ Simon &
Schuster
ISBN 0-671-622-390

YOUR CHILD'S GROWING
MIND—The first book to
integrate child development ,
whole brain reserach and learning
styles
by Jan Healy
Double Day & Company
ISBN 0-385-469-306

THE INFINITY WALK
Preparing Your Mind to Learn
by Deborah Sunbeck, Ph.D.
Jalmar Press
ISBN 1-880396-31-9

GROWING UP LEARNING
Focuses on sensory modalities-the
visual, auditory and tactile-
kinesthetic learners.
by Walter Barbe
Modern Learning Publishers
ISBN 1-567-620-884

IN THEIR OWN WAY
Discovering and encouraging
your child's personal learning
style, by T. Armstrong, Ph.D.
Jeremy P.Tarcher, Inc.
ISBN 0-87477-446-2

TEST YOUR I.Q. Third Ed.
by Alfred W. Munzert, Ph.D
Prentice Hall
ISBN 0-671-87459-4

TEACHING ELEMENTARY
STUDENTS THROUGH THEIR
INDIVIDUAL LEARNING
STYLES, by Rita Dunn
Allyn Bacon
ISBN 0-205-132-2

TEACHING STUDENTS TO
READ THROUGH THEIR
INDIVIDUAL LEARNING
STYLES, by Marie Cabo
Prentice Hall
ISBN 0-835-975-177

THE WAY THEY LEARN—
EVERY CHILD CAN
SUCCEED
by Cynthia Ulrich Tobias
Focus on the Family Publishing
ISBN 1-56179-253-5

A CHANCE TO LEARN
CIRRICULUM
A Chance to Grow, Inc.
New Visions School
1800 Second Street, N.E.
Minneapolis, MN 55418
(612) 706-5566

MUSIC FOR LEARNING

Accelerated Learning Solutions
6193 Summit Trail
Norcross, GA 30092
(770) 449-0640

LIND Institute
P.O. Box 14-487
San Francisco, CA 94114-0487
Relax w/the Classics
Learn w/the Classics
(415) 864-3396

VANILLA VOCABULARY
Visualized/Vocabulary
by Nanci Bell
Gander Publishing
ISBN 0-945-856-032

LEARNING FORUM®
Video and audio tape programs to
raise grades, increase motivation
and improve study skills. WCI
favorite…
Optima-learning Baroque
Music Vol. 1 & 2
Oceanside, CA
1-800-527-5321

100 WAYS TO IMPROVE
TEACHING WITH YOUR
VOICE AND MUSIC
by Don Campbell
Zephyr Press
ISBN 0-913-705-748

CREATING SUCESS: A
PROGRAM FOR
BEHAVIORALLY AND
ACADEMICALLY AT RISK
CHILDREN
by Terri Atkin
Innerchoice Publishing
ISBN 0-962-548-42

REACHING OUT TO
TROUBLED KIDS
15 Helpful Ways to Bridge the
Gap Between Parents, Teachers
and Kids, by Kathleen Fad, Ph.D.
(512) 328-7407 or
(303) 651-2829 Sopris West Pub.

LIVING WITH DIVORCE
Activities to Help Children Cope
with Difficult Situations (grades
5-9) by E. Garigan M.Ed.
Good Apple Publishing
ISBN 0866-53596-9
SAILING THROUGH THE
STORM—A Child's Journey
Through Divorce (ages 4-8)
by Edie Julik
Kidsail
ISBN 0-9642223-0-2

THE SINGLE MOTHER'S
BOOK—A practical guide to
managing your children, career,
home finances and everything
else, by Joan Anderson
Peach Tree Publishers
ISBN 0-934601-84-4

FEELINGS BURIED ALIVE
NEVER DIE (Revised)
by Karol Kuhn Truman
Olympus Distributing
ISBN 0-911207-02-3

DEPRESSION CURED AT
LAST
by Sherry Rogers, M.D.
Prestige
ISBN 1-887-202-013

LIFE SKILLS ACTIVITIES FOR
SPECIAL CHILDREN
by Darlene Mannix
Prentice Hall-Career
ISBN 0876285477

HELPING THE CHILD WHO
DOESN'T FIT IN
Solving the Puzzle of Social
Rejection, by S. Nowicki & M.
Duke, Peach Tree Publishing
ISBN 1-56145-025-1

SURVIVAL GUIDE FOR KIDS
WITH L.D.
(Learning Differences)
by G. Fisher & R. Cummings
Free Spirit Publishing
ISBN 0-915793-18-0

SURVIVAL STRATEGIES FOR
PARENTING YOUR A.D.D.
CHILD
Dealing with Obsessions,
Compulsions, Depression,
Explosive Behavior & Rage
by George T. Lynn
Underwood Books
ISBN 1-887424-19-9

TEACHING THE TIGER
A Handbook for Individuals
Involved in the Education of
Students with Attention Deficit
Disorders, Tourette Syndrome or
Obsessive-Compulsive Disorders
by M. Dornbush & S. Pruitt
Hope Press
ISBN 1-878267-34-5

DRIVEN TO DISTRACTION
by Hallowel, Simon and Schuster
ISBN 068-4801-280

HELP FOR THE
HYPERACTIVE CHILD
by William Crook, MD
Professional Books
Jackson, TN 38305
ISBN 0-933478-18-6

CRANIOSACRAL THERAPY
Vol. 1 (Instructive, indepth look.)
by John Upleger
Eastland Press
ISBN 0-939-616-017

OVERCOME CHALLENGES
The stories of five young people
who have overcome challenges.
One book from the EVERYDAY
HEROES book series
by Jill C. Wheeler
Abdo & Djh
ISBN 1-56239-700-1

UP FROM
UNDERACHIEVEMENT
How teachers, students, and
parents can work together to
promote student success
by Diane Heacox
Free Spirit Publishing
ISBN0-915793-35-0

PARENTS' MOST-ASKED
QUESTIONS ABOUT KIDS
AND SCHOOLS—A Leading
Educator Answers Concerns
About Your Children's
Education, by Cliff Schimmels
Focus On The Family
ISBN 0-89693-697-X

STRESS IN CHILDREN
How to Recognize, Avoid and
Overcome It, by Dr. Bettie Young
William Morrow
ISBN 0-87795-684-7

DR. SEHNERT'S NEW GUIDE
FOR STRESS MANAGEMENT
by Keith W. Sehnert
Augsburg Fantier's Publisher
ISBN 0-806-635-959

TOXIC CARPET III
by Glenn Beebe
P.O. Box 53344
Cincinnati, OH 45253

THE GIFT OF DYSLEXIA
Why some of the smartest people
can't read and how they can learn,
by Ronald Davis
A Perigee Book, Berkley Pub.
ISBN 0-929551-23-0

HELPING YOUR DYSLEXIC
CHILD—A step by step program
for helping your child improve
reading, writing, spelling,
comprehension and self-esteem
by Eileen Cronin
Prima Publishing
ISBN 1-559-582-901

ONE BRAIN: DYSLEXIC
LEARNING CORRECTION
AND BRAIN INTEGRATION
by Daniel Whiteside
Three In One Concepts
ISBN 0-918-993-008

HELP ME TO HELP MY
CHILD—A sourcebook for
parents of children with learning
disabilities, by Jill Bloom
Little Brown and Company
ISBN 0-316-09982-1

LIVING WITH AN ACTIVE
ALERT CHILD
by Linda Budd
Parenting Press
ISBN 094-399-0882

RAISING YOUR SPIRITED
CHILD
by Mary Sheedy Kurcinka
Harper Collins Publishers
ISBN 0-060-923-288

YOU MEAN I'M NOT LAZY,
CRAZY OR STUPID
by Kate Kelly
Simon & Schuster
ISBN 0-684-815-311

PUTTING ON THE BRAKES
Book and Activity Book
Activity Book for Young People
with ADHD
by Patricia Quinn M.D.
American Psychology
ISBN 094-535-4320

IF YOUR CHILD IS
HYPERACTIVE,
INATTENTIVE, IMPULSIVE,
DISTRACTIBLE . . .
Helping the ADD hyperactive
child with or without medications
by S. W. Garber, Ph.D.,
M. Daniels Coarbes, Ph.D.,and
Robyn Freedman Spizman
Villard Books
ISBN 0-394-572-05-X

BEYOND ADD: Hunting for
Reasons in the Past and Present
A look at the "Paradoxical
Effect" of being ADD
by Thom Hartmann
Underwood Books
ISBN 1-887424-12-1

ADD SUCCESS STORIES
A guide to fulfillment for families
with Attention Deficit Disorder
by Thom Hartmann
Underwood Books
ISBN 1-887424-03-2

THE ULTIMATE STRANGER
Hypo-Hyper Tactility Programs
by Delacato
Acad Thera
ISBN 0-878-794-468

SENSORY INTEGRATION
AND THE CHILD
by Jane Ayres
Western Press
ISBN 0-874-241-588

AUTISM TREATMENT GUIDE
A list of resources for autism
by Elizabeth Gerlach
Four Leaf Press, Eugene, OR
ISBN 0-9637578-0-6

BIOLOGICAL TREATMENTS
FOR AUTISM AND PDD
What's going on? What can you
do about it? Guide to current
research, by William Shaw Ph.D.
Contributions from Bernard
Rimland Ph.D. and more
Self-published in the U.S.A.
ISBN 0-9661238-0-8

SOCIAL SERIES: SOME
INTERPERSONAL SOCIAL
SKILL OBJECTIVES AND
TEACHING STRATEGIES FOR
PEOPLE WITH AUTISM
by Nancy Dalrymple Indiana
University Affiliated Program—
Institute for the Study of
Developmental Disabilities
2853 East Tenth Street
Bloomington, Indiana 47408-
2601 (812) 855-6508
FAX (812) 855-9630

THE NEW SOCIAL STORIES
BOOK—Carefully written for
children and adults with autism.
These stories help improve
mutual understanding for
individuals with autism and those
who work along side them.
Jenison Public Schools, edited by
Carol Gray & others
Future Horizons (817) 277-0727

FROM ANGER TO
FORGIVENESS
A practical guide to breaking the
negative power of anger
by Earnie Larsen
Ballantine Books
ISBN 0-345-37982-9

Cline/Fay Love & Logic Inc.
2207 Jackson Street
Golden, CO 80401
1-800-338-4065
*AVOIDING POWER
  STRUGGLES WITH KIDS
*THE VICTIM
*LOVE ME ENOUGH TO SET
  SOME LIMITS
*RAISING THE ODDS FOR
  RESPONSIBLE BEHAVIOR
*TROUBLE-FREE

TEENAGERS
*FOUR STEPS TO
  RESPONSIBILITY
*DIDN'T I TELL YOU TO
  TAKE OUT THE TRASH?

FREE FIGHT: CELEBRATING
YOUR RIGHT BRAIN
(right brainer in a left brain
world) by Barbara Vitale
Jalmar Press
ISBN 0-915-190-443
HOW TO TALK SO KIDS
WILL LISTEN & LISTEN SO
KIDS WILL TALK
Bring about more cooperation
from children than all the yelling
and pleading in the world
by Faber & Mazlish
Avon Book, NY
ISBN 0-380-57000-9

DUMBING US DOWN—THE
HIDDEN CURRICULUM OF
COMPULSARY SCHOOLING
by John Taylor Gatto
New Society Publishers
ISBN 0-865-712-31-X

RAISING POSITIVE KIDS IN A
NEGATIVE WORLD
by Zig Ziglar
Ballantine Books
ISBN 0-345-36188-1

THE ROAD LESS TRAVELED
by M. Scott Peck, M.D.
Author of The Diff. Drum
A Touchstone Book
Simon & Schuster
ISBN 0-671-24086-2

PRINCIPLE CENTERED
LEADERSHIP
by Stephen Covey
Fireside Publishers/Simon &
Schuster
ISBN 0-671-74910-2

SELLING OUT AMERICA'S
CHILDREN—How America Puts
Profits Before Values...
by David Walsh, Ph.D.
Fairview Press
ISBN 0-925190-47-0
THE DISCOVERY OF THE
CHILD, by Maria Montessor
Ballentine Books
ISBN 0-345-28009-1

THE DE-VALUING OF
AMERICA—The fight for our
culture and our children
by William J. Bennett
Summit Books
ISBN 0-671-68305-5

THE COMPLETE
ILLUSTRATED GUIDE TO
MASSAGE—Step by Step
Approach, by Stewart Mitchell
Barnes & Noble, NY
ISBN 0-760-70704-9

MAKING THE BEST OF
SCHOOLS (Parent Advocacy)
Gives adults confidence in
themselves as reformers and in
their children as scholars
by Jeannie Oakes
Yale University Press
ISBN 0-300-0512-39

COLLEGE ADMISSION
TESTING IN-A-FLASH
Flashcard series for
S.A.T.*/A.C.T. study.
1-402-727-8378

ILLUSTRATED
ENCYCLOPEDIA OF
ESSENTIAL OILS
by Julia Lawless
Barnes & Noble Books, NY
ISBN 1-566-19990-5

RESOURCES FOR PATTERNED LEARNERS

CHRISTOPHER LEE PUB.
1-800-822-6202
Lang. Arts, Math, Science,
Foreign Lang., & First Aide
—Flippers
CLP-394W **Eng. Grammer**
CLP-392W **Word Skills**
(Also available through Riggs)

INSTRUCTIONAL FAIR
1-800-253-5469
Grand Rapids, Michigan
Grammar
A Step by Step Approach

HEPNER AND HEPNER
CONSTRUCTION
1-800-257-1994
Box 7, 109 Wabasha
Warroad, MN 56763
Winston Grammar
Grocery Cart Math
Math It

TIMBERDOODLE
(360) 426-0672
E 1510 Spencer Lake Rd.
Shelton, WA 98584
(Math) Wrap-ups
Great for spacial skills.
Plastic strips with string.
Addition, Subtraction,
Multiplication, etc.

WEEKLY READER
1-800-446-3355
Map Skills Books
order #'s 32101, 32201,
32301, 32401

SAXON PUBLISHERS
(405) 329-7071
c/o Thompson Book
Depository
PO Box 60160
Oklahoma City, OK 73146
Saxon Math
(Can also be ordered from
Hepner and Hepner or others)

WEAVER UNIT STUDIES
LAKESHORE BASICS AND
BEYOND
1-800-421-5354
These fill in the dot quizes
develop test taking skills.
McCall Crabbs Reading-
Comprehension Quickies

MCDOUGAL-LITTELL
1-800-289-4490
18 Ballard Vail
Willmington, MN 01887
Daily Geography—12th
grade
Daily Analogies—2nd, 3rd,
4th grade
Daily Mathematics
1st Thesaurus

PHOENIX LEARNING
RESOURCES
1-800-221-1274
2349 Chaffee Dr.
St. Louis, MO 63146
Programmed Reading 1-2
Programmed Math
Both are great for "brain flips"

RESOURCES FOR PATTERNED LEARNERS

NATIONAL WRITING
INSTITUTE
(616) 684-5375
Perfect for Patterned Learners
Writing Strands (levels 1-7)
Reading Strands

BLUE BIRD PUBLISHING
(602) 831-6063
2266 So. Dobson Suite 275
Mesa, AZ 85202
Dr. Christman's -
Learn to Read

WILSON LANGUAGE
(508) 865-5699
175 W. Main St.
Millbury, MA 01527-1441
Wilson Student Readers
(Levels 1-12)
by Barbara A. Wilson

A BEKA BOOK
1-800-874-2352
#26468
My Blend and Word Sheets
A Handbook for Reading

WORLD BOOK
1-800-967-5325
Chicago, Illinois
Early Learning Set
Easy Readers

SHINING STAR
PUBLICATIONS
1-877-642-2316
Carthage, IL 62321-0299
Bible Codes and Messages
ISBN 0-86653-479-2

THE RIGGS INSTITUTE
1-800-200-4840
4185 SW 102nd Ave.
Beaverton, OR 97005
www.riggsinst.org
The Writing Road to
Reading
(Manual with Ayers list)
by Romalda Spalding
70 "Orton" phonogram
cards (letter sounds)
Flippers
McCall-Crabbs—
Comprehension Tests
Greek and Latin Flashcards
English From The Roots Up
(Help for Reading, Writing,
Spelling, and S.A.T. Scores)

CRITICAL THINKING
BOOKS & SOFTWARE
1-800-458-4849
PO Box 448
Pacific Grove, CA 93950
Thinking Skills
Book 1-Q42, Book 2-Q43

ALPHA OMEGA
PUBLICATIONS
1-800-622-3070
www.home-schooling.com
300 North McKemy Avenue
Chandler, AZ
Life-pac Total Cirriculum
Packages
Rainbow Fraction Tiles
Fraction Stax™
Geoboard Teachers Manual
(Rubber bands make shapes)

RESOURCES FOR PATTERNED LEARNERS

OUR SUNDAY VISITOR
1-800-348-2440
200 Noll Plaza
Huntington, IN 46750
I Am Special Series

TEACHING AND
LEARNING COMPANY
(217) 357-2591
204 Buchanan Street
PO Box 10
Carthage, IL 62321-0010
**My Favorite President-
Poster Papers**

CIRRICULUM
ASSOCIATES
(800) 225-0248
www.cahomeschool.com
P.O. Box 2001
No. Billerica, MA 01862-0901
Quick-word Handbooks
Primary Reader's Theatre
Working Phonics
Super Sonic Phonics

TROLL
1-800-929-8765
Easy Reading High Interest
Famous People Books, etc.

EDUCATIONAL INSIGHTS
1-800-933-3277
Dominguez Hills, CA
Match Frame (need 1 w/books)
Match Frame Books (ages 6-10)
EI-4452 (beg. Phonics)
EI-4453 (adv. Phonics)
EI4458 (general educ. skills)
EI4457 (matching)

**GeoSafari-
Learning Computer/cards**
for ages 8 and up
GeoSafari Early Learning

HIGH NOON BOOKS
1-800-422-7249
20 Commercial Boulevard
Novato, CA 94949-6191
Reading Comp. Series-boxes
Half "N" Design and Color
Eye-Hand Coord. Boosters
Fine Tuning

GROLIER ENTERPRISES, **1-
800-955-9877**
Sherman Turnpike
Danbury, CT 06810
**Now You Can Read Bible
Stories** (Easy Readers)

DISCOVERY TOYS
Call: 1-800-426-4777 for an
Educational Consultant
Rainbows, Rabbits, & Roses
(Phonic/Alphabet-Floor Puzz.)
Think It Through Tiles
Think It through Books
(books go with tile set)
www.discoverytoysinc.com

FOCUS ON THE FAMILY
1-800-A-FAMILY
Colorado Spring, CO
The Way They Learn
No Two Alike
by Cynthia Ulrich Tobias
Both books are about learning
styles and teaching children.

RESOURCES FOR PATTERNED LEARNERS

WAYNE STATE
UNIVERSITY PRESS
(313) 577-6120
The Leonard N. Simons
Building
5959 Woodward Ave.
Detroit, MI 48202
**Let's Read:
A Linguistic Approach**
by Leonard Bloomfield
ISBN 0-8143-1115-6
**June Brown's Guide to Let's
Read** Parent/Teacher Manual
by June Brown Garner
ISBN 0-8143-1690-5

SCHOOL ZONE
PUBLISHING CO.
1-800-253-0564
Grand Haven, Michigan
49417
**Short Vowels 1-3
Long Vowels 1-3
Phonics Review 2-3
English 2
English 3-4**

SELF-TALK INSTITUTE
1-800-982-8196
Shad Helmstetter's
Self-Talk Cassettes:
Self-esteem for Older Kids

LADYBIRD BOOKS,INC.
**The Ladybird Book of
Tables and Other Measures**
A Quick and Easy Math
Reference
ISBN 0-7214-0663-7

**Slow and Steady Get Me
Ready**
260 weekly developmental
activities from birth to age 5
by June R. Oberlander
Bio-Alpha
Fairfax Station Virginia
ISBN 0-9622322-0-3

EDU-KINESTHETICS
1-805-650-3303
Ventura, CA
Resources for
whole brain learning
Brain Gym™
by Paul Dennison Ph.D.

BARNES & NOBLE
OR YOUR LOCAL
BOOKSELLER
www.barnesandnoble.**com**

BOOKS TO READ:

Unicorns are Real
A Right Brain Approach
To Learning
by Barbara Vitale
Jalmar Press
ISBN 091-519-035-4

**The New Reading Teacher's
Book of Lists**
by E. Bernard Fry, Ph.D.,
Dona Lee Foutoukidis, Ed.D.,
and J. Kress Polk, M.A.
Prentice Hall, Inc.

RESOURCES FOR PATTERNED LEARNERS

Books To Read Continued

The Learning Revolution
by Gordon Dryden & J. Vos
ISBN 1-880396-34-3

**Smart Moves Why
Learning Is Not All In Your
Head**
by Carla Hannaford, Ph.D.
ISBN 0-915556-27-8

The Dominance Factor
by Carla Hannaford
ISBN 0-915556-31-6

The Gift of Dyslexia
(Newly Revised Edition)
Why Some of the Smartest
People Can't Read and How
They Can Learn——The
Revolutionary New Method of
Correcting Dyslexia and Other
Learning Disorders
By Ronald D. Davis
ISBN 0-399-52293-X

Homeschool Burnout
by Raymond S. Moore
ISBN 0-943497-35-3
Wolgemuth & Hyatt

Teaching
**A First Dictionary of
Cultural Literacy**
(or individual grade level books)
by E.D. Hirsch Jr.

Most of the books and
learning tools listed, can be
used with Patterned Learners
of all ages.

INSTRUCTIONAL FAIR
1-800-253-5469
First Grade in Review
(other grades also available)
Math, Reading, Science,
Spelling
Language, Social Studies
A Homework Booklet.
Grand Rapids, Michigan

**The Word-A-Day For
Homework Book**
A Word-A-Day approach to
vocabulary enrichment for
elementary school children
by Marlene Glaus
Take My Word For It Books
4575 W. 80th St. Circle #242
Bloomington, MN 55437
(612) 831-5448

Where is Thumpkin?
Science, art, language, math,
motor skills, drama, etc.
Connected curriculm w/songs
by Pam Schiller
Gryphone House
Mt. Rainier, Maryland
(301) 779-620

**Developing The
Early Learner**
Perception Publications
(602) 997-2292
Strengthen your child's
perceptual foundations.
Four levels of learning.
by Simone Bibeau, M.A. Sp. Ed.
1814 West Selodon Lane
Phoenix, AZ 85021